Narratives of Remembrance

Introduction

Great War poems.

1. The same old soldiers walking along the same old skyline
2. Dead hand through the sandbags reaching out for the cream-and-white butterfly
3. mud/water under duckboards/mud/rats scamper in starshell darkness/mud/smell of shit and rotting bodies/mud/resting your sweaty forehead on the sandbags OVER THE TOP the first men in the lunar landscape.
4. 'What did you do to the Great Whore, Daddy?'
5. Poppies slightly out-of-focus and farmcarts bringing in the peaceful dead.
6. The ghost of Wilfred Owen selling matches outside the Burlington Arcade.
7. Seafog. Red flaring lights from the shorebatteries. The roar of shells rattle of machineguns. Water running in the bilges. My feet slipping on the damp cobbles of the quayside.
8. DON'T BE VAGUE – BLAME GENERAL HAIG.
9. four white feathers clutched in a blood-stained envelope
10. a skull nesting in a bed of wild strawberries/boots mouldering green with fungus/saplings thrusting through rusting helmets/sunken barges drifting full of leaves down autumn rivers.

Adrian Henri[1]

The above text figures among poems resolutely committed to living and loving in the now, a slightly desperate bid for minimalist gratification which has been held typical of the sixties.[2] To achieve even that modest goal, young people had to get rid of parents' war-ridden past, lingering on evocatively in the shape of memories, objects and images, but, as another Mersey poem makes clear, rejected in its public construction.[3] Thirty years later, the past seems to face a worse enemy than rebellious youth, namely the present; the bombardment of ceaseless, multiple, and simultaneous information by the electronic media crowds out all other claims to attention, threatening the near-demise of a historical consciousness and, with that loss, a life determined by whim, flux, and chance.[4] It also spells the loss of what is arguably the last definitional anchor for a meaningful concept of 'identity,' personal or collective, namely a continuous relation to the past.

The Cartesian reliance upon the priority of the self and thus the validity of the personal cognitive endeavour have been questioned, not only by an increasing failure to discover metaphysical moorings for that priority, but also by the twentieth-century attack on the traditional notion of the self as unified and conscious of itself. Freud exposed identity as a largely uncontrollable interplay between forces hypothesised to account for erratic behaviour which was not, however, aberrant, but in fact representative of irrational man; Lacan went on to view the wholeness of an "imaginary self" as illusory, the actual 'self' being "perpetually in flux."[5] At present, theorists tend to replace the 'self' – a soul anchored in God, or the autonomous Cartesian thinker – with an externally constituted 'subject', unstable, yet rigorously determined, since selfhood is viewed as a function of ideological or linguistic determinants.

This deterministic vision of man (as well as Lyotard's equally nightmarish romance of liberating madness) may, however, be countered by a view of *man as story-teller*:

> In the process of narration, discrete moments and acts are contextualized: they are enmeshed in history. Historical narrative contextualization is crucial to human understanding ... [N]arrative ... anticipates an end (which may be revised), and aspires to order (which may be provisional). Narrative conceptualization enables the creation of a revisable, provisional, but more or less readable self, and facilitates the experience of self-continuity

through time. [The] human capacity for self-revision, or more precisely the capacity to reconceptualize the self through revision of narratives of selfhood [spells] a degree of personal autonomy. [Such narration makes] the human subject [an] agent of both personal and social change.[6]

Narratives interrogate and renegotiate relations between self and its constitutive cultural and linguistic forces, and narrating the past is a crucial part of that empowering project.

The rules by which narratives change are similar to those of memory, about which Plato observed that memory has more to do with forgetting than with remembering. The pragmatic selectiveness and transformations of memory by which a "necessary past" is produced have increasingly come into focus as determinants of identity, individual and collective.

The editorial operation of personal memory or institutionally organised remembrance inevitably compromises the empirical truth, what *really* happened. Art and memory are long-standing partners in editing the empirical, mimetic fiction often being indistinguishable from reports of fact. Below, Lars Ole Sauerberg discusses the resultant critical quandary and proposes to resolve it by addressing texts on the basis of function rather than by their metaphorical or metonymical relation to empirical reality, a strategy reminiscent of functionalist criteria within source criticism employed by an influential branch of historians.[7] The imaginative transformations of the past is taken up by the author Helen Dunmore, whose description of her research for the novel *Zennor in Darkness* highlights the complexities of recovering the world of WWI, yet also poses an affinity between an author and a particular period or writer; a dynamic which suggests that an artist's present-day engagement with the past subsumes two constructions of time, one liniar, one typological. The value of the (re)created past as a transfiguring reflection of and upon the present is the theme of Marianne Børch, who further ponders the value of the historicising perspective built into written as against oral records.

The metaphor of remembrance has its dangers, memory's narratives arguably furnishing metaphors rather than metonomies of reality. So, while the slanted nature of political and individual remembrance has long been acknowledged, the historian has usually invoked a commitment to the empirical and a spirit of scholarly disinterestedness which make his endeavour essentially different from (other forms of) reminiscence. Recent decades have brought heated debate about the implications of history as narrative, since narrative's aesthetic and ethical coherence inevitably compromises empirical correspondence. That history employs narrative does not, however, turn history into fiction, argues Jens Rahbek Rasmussen in a passionate defence of history; history's narratives of remembrance are "a range of interpretations" of precious facts, to whose preservation the historian remains deeply committed: once lost, no narration will save them.

The possibility of different interpretations of always incomplete facts has been enthusiastically embraced by communities and students dissatisfied with available constructions. New historical narratives foreground feminist, ethnic, or national interests, or break with dominant narratives as simply obsolete, shaped by assumptions and needs no longer relevant. Even historical narratives which are in a sense 'true to the facts' demand the revision of elaboration and complication; new narratives arise out of underexposed or rejected material and often significantly modify available 'master' marratives, whether generated by academics or governments. While such 'new' pasts are far from fictional, yet they are constructed, as the new historical narrative historicises previous ones. Below, Nils Arne Sørensen demonstrates how WWI came to acquire its enduring mythical value for modern Britain, suggesting that recovering the facts of the Great War may well happen at the cost of its emotional value. Eve Patten takes up the after-images of WWII to show how its representations, actively stage-managed by politicians and the media, obscured a diversity of individual and regional experiences, and are still enlisted to serve widely different political interests. Remaining illusions about a simple connection between facts and their representation are finally shattered by David Mccrone's demonstration that the construct of a Scottish Heritage is shaped more by a complex network of present-day interests – political, economic, and sentimental – than by an interest in the actual past or a Scottish identity rooted in, and authenticated by, that past.

Memories are made of gold, and, as suggested by Nils Arne Sørensen, subjecting them to the glare of academic scrutiny may well buy stale truth at the cost of live value. However, recovering the reality behind remembrances, as well as laying bare the alchemy by which empirical matter is turned into virtual gold, has its own satisfactions, both those of the search and those of discoveries that allow at least provisional closure and wholeness. Thus, while possibly shattering treasured myths and dissecting their subtle production, the historian, literary scholar, or cultural historian is herself engaged upon a stimulating, quasi-romantic quest.[8] We hope that the articles in this book will stimulate in readers a desire to study, generate and share new narratives of remembrance similar to that which led to the present publication.[9]

Notes

1. *The Mersey Sound* (Harms.: Penguin, 1967), p. 24
2. Patricia Waugh, *Harvest of the Sixties* (Oxford, Oxford UP, 1995), pp. 24-36.
3. "Why Patriots are a Bit Nuts in the Head," Roger McGough, *The Mersey Sound*, p. 73.
4. See Steven Connor, *The English Novel in History, 1950-95* (London: Routledge, 1996), pp. 28 ff., who in analysing the experience of Saleem Sinai in Rushdie's *Midnight's Children* is reminded of the experience described by Jean Beaudrillard: "as 'the absolute proximity, the total instantaneity of things, the feeling of no defense, no retreat. It is the end of interiority and intimacy, the overexposure and transparency of the world which traverses ... without obstacle'" (p. 32).
5. *Columbia Dictionary of Modern Literary and Cultural Criticism*, ed. Joseph Childers & Gary Hentzi (New York: Columbia University Press, 1995); entries on "Identity" (p. 148) and "Subject" (p. 292).
6. Kim L. Worthington, *Self as Narrative* (Oxford: Clarendon Press, 1996), pp. 14-5.
7. Represented by, for instance, H.P.Clausen and Helge Paludan. Thanks to Nils Arne Sørensen for alerting me to this.
8. The quest may be motivated by a shared interest in the past, but clearly it takes different forms, as do subsequent travelogues. From among a variety of conventions for setting up notes and bibliographies, two have been accepted in this book as equally clear and informative, one predominant among historians, the other prevalent among writers on literature.
9. Desire initiates the quest, but to arrange for sharing and exchanging the spoils takes more than desire. The editor wishes to thank British Council and Odense

University for funding the conference that occasioned five out of the seven present articles Narratives of Remembrance, organized by associate professors Nils Arne Sørensen, Leo Hoye, and Marianne Børch.

D H Lawrence and the First World War: The Writing of *Zennor in Darkness*

Helen Dunmore

Before I discuss the research and the writing of this novel I'd like to give background which will suggest what led me to write about this particular time and this particular man. I want to argue that there is often a 'fit' between the novelist and her or his subject matter, which makes writing about a historical period very much more than a matter of cool decision and subsequent research. In a sense, that particular period has already knitted itself into the writer's life *before* the novel is begun.

When I was fourteen, my family moved to Nottingham, and there I attended Nottingham High School for Girls, which as you may know is directly opposite the school which D H Lawrence attended, Nottingham High School for Boys. Naturally enough, there was quite a bit of contact between the High School girls and the High School boys. One of the first things I remember hearing about the school was that D H Lawrence had been a pupil there. I think that when one is young, the moment of realisation that a historical figure, a famous writer, had an existence which may be measured against one's own is extremely powerful. D H Lawrence, the famous writer, the author who had been responsible for the Lady Chatterley trial, had also been a child here, had walked into the school across the road, had done his examinations there, thought this or that about the place and the masters. When he was spoken of, it was in that complicated, half-ironic, half-envious tone in which local communities speak of their famous sons and daughters - particularly of those who are notorious as well as famous.

The proximity of Nottingham High School for Boys, the closeness of the landscapes which Lawrence wrote about, gave an added edge to our studies of *Sons & Lovers* or *The Rainbow*. We felt that we were in the same world, and empathised with Lawrence's accounts of love, imperfect, tormented relationships, and the ruthless drive of the adolescent to become an independent self. We recognised the snags of grief and guilt which had caught at Lawrence's imagination. We felt for Miriam, yet we found her maddening.

Ken Russell's film of *Women in Love* confirmed this passion. The film idealised free women who were at the same time deeply enmeshed in relationships with men, and who defined themselves through these men. This was very much the ethos of our own time (the late sixties). But later, on reaching the University of York, I would argue vehemently in seminars against Lawrence's sexism. The wave of feminism was just breaking on England, and this led to a renewed and more critical focus on Lawrence. But I could never be doctrinaire about him for long. He was simply too good a writer, too subtle, too sensitive, too ready to slip the mesh of a reader's preconceptions. At the time I was at York, F R Leavis was a visiting professor, giving lectures and seminars. The repercussions of his Cambridge battles were vague gossip in our ears, but it was moving to hear him speak so warmly of our new university, of the way we were learning, of the freshness of the vision being offered to us. Leavis was clearly a remarkable, though a very fragile figure: combative, complex, urgent. I was already familiar with his criticism of Lawrence, but to hear him speak brought again that curiously vital sensation of immediacy, proximity; of history being something which *does not finish* but which continually feeds and revitalises our own experience. We understand history when we have sufficient experience to pick up its reverberations. I chose the study of Lawrence as one of my options at York, and began to read more widely, exploring the travel literature, the letters, biography and criticism.

I believe that latency is a very important and insufficiently recognised aspect of creativity. Sometimes all the material appears to be in place, yet it is years until a trigger sets off the process, and a novel or poem is begun. I continued to read and re-read Lawrence, more casually, without any sense of ultimate purpose. When I was twenty-three I went to live in the south-west of England, and on frequent stays in Cornwall became very familiar with West Penwith, with Zennor, St Ives, the coastline and the unique landscape there. I already knew the story of Lawrence's wartime experiences there from 'The Nightmare' section of *Kangaroo,* but I was not keenly interested or curious. If anything, I would have criticised a note of hysteria, or over-reaction in this section of the novel. Surely, compared to the war experiences of other writers and poets, Lawrence's were not so very terrible? It is a question of how one reads, again. There were things there which I simply did not pick up. But in 1991 several things came together.

First of all, there was the Gulf War. Like many people, I was opposed to the way in which this conflict was resolved. There were eerie similarities of scale and strategy with the First World War: the constant threat of poison gas; the huge Iraqi call-up, often of untrained men; the digging in of this army in trenches along the Kuwaiti border; the blind conviction of rectitude on both sides. And most chilling of all, the new ways in which language began to be used, and what this change of use reflected. News broadcasts and analysis programmes moved forward on the stepping-stones of huge, unquestioned assumptions. The demonisation of the enemy progressed rapidly, and so did the sense that it was unpatriotic to oppose any ' necessary measure' and that those who did were fundamentally disloyal. A mental shift had to be prepared, so that the fate of the Iraqi conscript army would come to seem not only necessary but desirable.

I do not know exactly why all this sent me straight back to 'The Nightmare' section of *Kangaroo,* and to a realisation that what Lawrence was writing about was not an exaggeration, but an attempt to dramatise this climate at once stifling and terrifying. I knew a lot about the history and literature of the First World War, so in a sense that knowledge was waiting, in place. One April evening a fellow tutor at a residential writing course chanced to say to me how surprising it was to find a woman writer who had such respect for Lawrence's work. We had been talking very briefly and generally about the travel writing. At that moment the whole idea for the novel rose into my mind - or rather, I first allowed myself to see what was already there, latent, fully formed.

This is why when people ask about my research, as they often do when a novel has a historical and biographical basis, I say that it was not a matter of simply going away and reading up about the

First World War, about Lawrence, or about Cornwall. It was more a matter of making connections, and of a surge of creative electricity which brought all these aspects of a potential novel into a vital relationship with one another. Fortunately, a great deal of the reading was already done, and it was a question of re-reading more purposefully, and then using this reading as a pointer to new material which I wanted to discover. I explored newspapers, diaries, privately published accounts by non-commissioned soldiers (in which I was especially interested), and accounts of the changes in women's social and economic position during the First World War. I looked at collections of photographs, visited the Imperial War Museum, spoke to museum staff, listened to taped autobiographies. In terms of the Lawrence reading, it meant a very sharp, close focus on that period, and on accounts, diaries and memoirs by contemporaries such as Katherine Mansfield, Catherine Carswell, John Middleton Murry, Virginia Woolf, Cynthia Asquith and many others. Naturally, Lawrence's own letters were invaluable. I also wanted to look at the impact that the stay in Zennor had on Lawrence's later life, even though I would not be writing about this. I felt that it would affect the way that I dramatised those months of wartime.

The visits I now made to Zennor and St Ives were purposeful, linking what I already knew of landscape, atmosphere, people, customs and the use of the Cornish language to the history of Zennor and St Ives during the First World War. I needed to soak myself in that period, its habits, rhythms, the way people lived, ate, bought food, the way rationing affected the area, the way conscription impinged on this remote part of Britain. In a sense, the task of a novelist in her research is to know much more than she will ever need to include. It is like furnishing a house fully. so that you can walk around it without really noticing things, in the way that one does in daily life. Only in this way can a casual allusion fall just as it should. In the same way, it was vital not to be over-eager to cram in information about Lawrence, unless this was important to the movement of the narrative. I wanted to create something seamless, something which would convince through the subtle accumulation of detail rather than through listings of facts.

I was fortunate in that the Zennor area has changed so little, compared to many other areas of rural or urban Britain. Bronze Age field patterns are still there, as Lawrence observed them: the granite hedges, the loggan stone of these fields could not be easily moved, even if any farmer were so misguided as to try to get rid of his best protection against soil erosion and Atlantic weather. In this part of West Penwith, it hasn't been possible to tear up hedges and introduce those prairie fields which have changed the landscape of East Anglia, for example, since the second World War. The landscape of Zennor is a granite landscape, characterised as much by sea and sky as by earth, and not easily altered. The same families have lived there for generations. Zennor has no aristocratic 'big house' or squirearchy. Instead, local society consists of farms and cottages scattered over a big parish which runs down to the sea and up to the downs. Quicks, Thomases, Berrymans, Nankervises, Osborns, Hockings recur again and again, and the churchyard in Zennor is full of them. This is a close, intimately interrelated web which survived mass emigration after the closure of the tin mines, and is surviving modernisation. Through this web memories of the Lawrences are handed down, as are every other incident of note, from the wrecking of a ship to a cow getting into a parlour. In some cases these memories had been so polished by retelling that they had lost spontaneity. For example, Stanley Hocking's memories of the Lawrences had been recounted, taped, transcribed etc. In other cases they were perfunctory, a world of meaning concealed in a few words, as when Granny Griggs (Alison Symons' grandmother) remarked that 'She always found Lawrence a gentleman, though there were plenty who disliked him.' Interestingly, after the publication of *Zennor in Darkness*, further sources opened up. I was sent books such as Alison Symons' *Tremedda Days,* which not only contains some family memories of contact with the Lawrence's, but also gives a very full picture of farming life in Zennor during the First World War.

    I had to draw on sources such as farming diaries, dialect collections, guides to place names and Cornish language remnants in dialect. I visited the cottage where D H Lawrence and Frieda lived. As I accumulated material, I had to remember that in the end I was writing a novel and must take control of and shape the material rather than letting research become obsessive.

    As you can imagine, the supreme requirement was an imaginative immersion in the time, its language, its idiom, its tension, and in a society which was closed, unique, rich and particular. What was life like for the family of a small draper in St Ives, or for a farmer with little land, or for a young woman, my female protagonist, whose personal destiny was crossing a tide of the huge changes made by that war in the futures of young women? Clare Coyne had to be hungry. She was hungry for what was outside her own experience, while also being a creature of that experience. Like Lawrence himself, she is a half-and-half, the daughter of an educated man and an uneducated mother who has died and left her to the care of her father and the powerful clan of her mother's family. She has artistic talent, buried by her father's use of it for accurate, botanical drawing. She is practical, sharp-witted, intelligent and never remotely self-pitying. When she meets Lawrence and Frieda, she is shown a way of life which has never entered her reckoning before: impoverished, but self-sufficient, openly emotional, treating the making of art as hard, necessary work, and expecting to live by it, however poorly. The Lawrences made homes in cottages which a labourer's wife would have considered poor, yet they covered them with rich cloth and pictures and odd bits of brilliant colour.

Then there was Frieda's Germanness. Frieda has suffered greatly from racial stereotyping. During the First World War, German women married to British men were known as 'Hunwives', and were mistrusted as potential enemies. There was a spy fever which led to brutal and ludicrous actions against those suspected of furthering the German cause. Frieda, with her German aristocratic background, her contempt for conventional appearances and morality, her maiden surname (von Richthofen), and her powerful physical presence, did not and could not belong in a small rural community in wartime.

I wanted the novel to be incisive, almost funny at points as all these cultural collisions take place, and yet also lyrical and potentially tragic. So I contrasted the figure of Lawrence with Clare Coyne's cousin, the young non-commissioned officer who is recalled for officer training. John William is a soldier against whom Clare measures the Lawrences, but he is also a young man so mentally battered by life in the trenches that there is very little point of communication between him and civilians any more. He cannot be reached, even by the cousin who loves him. He is caught between two worlds, and in the end he can survive in neither.

In this novel, it was vital for me to capture each character's distinctive rhythm of speech. The rhythms of Lawrence's speech are fluid, idiosyncratic and show the layers of his experience, from boyhood in Nottingham, to marriage to a native German-speaker, to a life of roaming from continent to continent. His speech leaps from the pages of his letters and his novels. But each character in *Zennor in Darkness* needed an individual voice. There are the subtle variations of diction from person to person. There are the pomposities of the small business man, the eager, flaring speech of Clare Coyne, the reticence of Nan, the dry humour of Clare's cousin Hannah, the gossippy voices of certain onlookers to the main action. I wanted to suggest the period through the shaping of speech. Certain phrases will give the right flavour without appearing over-researched. Contractions were not used in the same way in 1917 as they are now. In addition, local speech patterns would inform even the speech of an educated person in the area of Zennor and St Ives. Among farming communities, Cornish words and phrases were still in everyday use, even though the language was no longer spoken as a whole. All this had to be suggested quite subtly, through the texture of the novel's dialogue and interior monologue.

I think that one of the strongest affinities I feel for Lawrence are to do with his sense of place. His landscapes are not settings, but organic parts of the action. This is very much how I feel about landscape myself, and about the reciprocal relationship that grows between place and people. Response between a person and a landscape is not only a matter of belonging there; I was struck powerfully by the way Lawrence wrote of the Zennor landscape to friends, how he sent them boxes of wild flowers, how immediately and passionately he felt an affinity between himself and this place. And yet he did not belong, and the place almost destroyed hirn. After the Zennor years, Lawrence set his face against the England which he felt had misjudged him and was no longer a place he could call his home. After 1919 he never lived permanently in England again, although no other writer loves the English landscape more passionately than Lawrence, or brings it more dazzlingly to life in his writing.

Private Memory, Public Recollection: Narratives of the Second World War

Eve Patten

In 1882, the ethnographer Ernest Renan described the soul of a nation as the possession of a rich legacy of memories and the desire to perpetuate the values of that inheritance. In the formation of nationality, he suggested, the process of remembering is more valuable than customs posts and frontiers, for the past provides a common heritage which transcends differences of race and language. 'A heroic past, great men, glory', he wrote, 'this is the social capital upon which one bases a national idea.'[1]

Renan's definition of nationhood has provided a springboard for many subsequent investigations into the strategies and ironies surrounding our constructions of a national past. The extent to which the nation can be 'read' as a product of sustaining narratives and the transformation of the past into such narratives has been explored in this context by various writers including Benedict Anderson, Homi Bhabha and Joep Leerssen.[2] In terms of Britain, the political, social and aesthetic parameters of remembrance have been addressed most extensively by Raphael Samuel, whose two-volume *Theatres of Memory* offers a magisterial treatment of memory as historically conditioned and inherently revisionist; a dynamic and creative force within the contexts of heritage and historiography.[3] From such material, we have gained an intense awareness of the past as a potent resource, and of 'History' as W. H. Auden's 'Great Organiser', continually entwining our individual identities in a collective consciousness.

My interest in this paper lies in the idea that Renan's concept of a national memory based on solidarity and consent is achievable only at the expense of private memory and perhaps dissent. I shall focus on the way in which the particular 'narrative' of the Second World War can be located in the intersection of private memory and public recollection, and I want to pose two questions in relation to this. First, and most obviously, if the war itself was experienced at the time on both an individual and a national level, how did the two levels relate to each other, and how did the individual story merge into the fabric of the national epic? Here we must address the powerful machinery of popular culture and the media, through which the *re-presentation* of events began to take precedence over the reality.[4] Secondly, I want to explore the way in which the narratives of private memory are appropriated over time by the strategic demands of public recollection, and to ask how contemporary Britain has managed (or stage-managed) the memory of the Second World War. The 1995 'Victory in Europe' or VE Day anniversary celebrations held throughout the United Kingdom were a vivid manifestation of the way in which a media-driven version of the past serves to displace contemporary grievances, enforcing a dominant narrative which is highly resistant to alternative readings. The phenomenon suggests that as Renan observed, a nation remembers many things, but it must also forget.[5] In the attempt to forge a national consensus through appeals to the past, it would seem that collective memory is frequently and necessarily accompanied by collective amnesia.

It could be argued that everybody has their own personal 'narrative of remembrance', even those who were born many years after the war ended. The stories related by parents and grandparents, and the images transmitted by literature, music and film, create access to a second or third-hand version of a world of ration books and powdered egg, whale meat and black market sugar, blackout curtains and garden dug-out shelters, the haunting sound of the air-raid siren and the first taste of post-war ice-cream. Within some families and communities, such as my own, such images have a strong currency, but even those from outside what one might see as a direct inheritance of wartime experience have absorbed something of this material, simply as a result of the way in which it permeates contemporary culture.

While individual details might differ somewhat, I would suggest that for many, the opening of the 'war narrative' coincides with one of two events: the trauma and excitement of evacuation, as thousands of children from British cities were relocated with families in the comparative safety of the countryside, and the radio broadcast of 11.15am on September 3rd, 1939, in which the British Prime Minister, Neville Chamberlain, gravely informed the people of Britain that they were now officially at war. Both experiences have made the transition from private to public recollection, in that both have entered Britain's literary and cinematic culture as the recognised metonyms of wartime and as enduring linchpins of national memory. Both represent the reality so persuasively that any divergence from the formula they provide is immediately noticeable, as Alan Bennett implies in the opening essay of his autobiographical collection *Writing Home*, in which he tells of his own experience of the outbreak of war in terms of its deviation from, rather than conformity to, the national norm:

> I was five when the war started, and Monday 4 September 1939 should have been my first day at school; but that was not to be. I wish I could record our family as gathered anxiously round the wireless, as most were at eleven o'clock that Sunday morning, but I already knew at least at the age of five that I belonged to a family that without being in the least bit remarkable or eccentric, yet managed never to be quite like other families. If we had been, my brother and I would have been evacuated with all the other children the week before, but Mam and Dad hadn't been able to face it. So, not quite partaking in the national mood and, as ever, unbrushed by the wings of history, Mr Chamberlain's broadcast found us on a tram going down Tong Road into Leeds. Fearing the worst, my parents had told my brother and me that we were all going out into the country that day and we were to have a picnic – something I had hitherto only come across in books.[6]

The first point to be made here, which Bennett's allusion to the 'national mood' conveys, is that the war was a mass experience for the British population, and that memories of its outbreak in 1939 are already collectivised, in a sense, by the uniformity which was imposed on social and cultural life. But more significantly, Bennett's sentiments on *not* being part of the whole ('I wish I could record...') suggest that the dominant experience also gained a kind of authenticity within a collective cultural consciousness, acquiring a narrative credibility which any alternative experience inevitably lacks.

Even autobiographical accounts of the war therefore, within which one might expect individuality, tend to observe certain archetypal configurations in their attempts to communicate both the reality of a collective experience, and the authority of a collective representation. One might compare Bennett's recollections with those of the British film-maker John Boorman, who scripted and directed his 1987 film *Hope and Glory* as an autobiographical account of growing up in a semi-suburban London street in the shadow of the war.[7] Boorman makes it clear that for the children of his generation the bizarre circumstances which war brought about were more exciting and liberating than traumatic, but he also creates a narrative which, as autobiography, is very definitely collective rather than individual. The film emphasises from the beginning the formulaic lifestyle of London's suburban families: as the news of war breaks in Chamberlain's broadcast, it is noted in voice-over that 'all the lawnmowers stopped at once'. Every family in the street is shown to live according to the same domestic timetable and rituals, in the mowing of the lawn or the drinking of tea, and it is implied synechdochically that the entire nation in 1939 is completely homogenous, so that any individual experience is entirely representative, and the ordinary valorised above the idiosyncratic.

What Boorman sets up as individual memory in the film therefore, is simultaneously presented as public property. But the film also illustrates the way in which the experience of war is collectivised through popular culture and media. In the opening sequence the camera moves from a selection of family photographs to the cinema-screen, on which newsreel telling of worsening international relations shares a platform with a Hollywood Western, as though to suggest that *representations* of the world, and indeed of the family itself, are becoming inextricable from the reality of identity and experience. In the same way, the film suggests that the media will increasingly take control of the war narrative. An early scene depicts the family gathered around the wireless set as the Prime Minister broadcasts to the nation, the father reading a newspaper and the youngest daughter, unaware of the unfolding crisis, singing a popular war-time song. We are introduced to the idea that any access to the 'events' of the war is not direct but mediated, channelled through a series of institutions and systems which narrativise the experience on the public's behalf.

In such scenes Boorman's film offers a reminder of the extent to which the experience of war in 1939 was accompanied and formulated by a strengthening mass culture. Whereas in the war of 1914-18, the transmission of news material to print and screen would sometimes take several days, the representation of the Second World War was almost immediate, as media technology grew in sophistication and impact.[8] Events at home and abroad were shaped as 'narratives' through reporting, interpreting, editing, headlining and photographic illustration, and then made available to the general public through the daily newspaper and the cinema newsreel. Life in wartime Britain had an instantaneous, accessible popular culture soundtrack through a flourishing showbusiness world and a lifestyle representation through the imagery of commercial advertising. Even the intrusion of the government's public information campaigns into almost every aspect of domestic life, from cookery to childcare, created representative images of standard wartime behaviour. And so the private world was forced into a collective experience, in that the war was lived through the apparatus of popular media culture, and the population thus bound together in the creation of a national myth of self, falling in love, as Raphael Samuel describes it, with its own representation on screen or in print.[9]

It was particularly the operations of the press which enabled the individual to be drawn into the common experience. In her wartime novel, *The Heat of the Day* (1948), the writer Elizabeth Bowen describes how one of her characters, Louie, becomes dependent on newspapers to create not only an appropriate version of the war, but also an acceptable version of herself. Having started to read the daily press, which decides every event's importance for her by the size of print in which it is reported, Louie is delighted to find herself accepted into the secure community of the newspaper's world:

> [H]ow inspiring was the variety of the true stories, which made the war seem almost human, people like her important, and life altogether like it was once. But is was from the articles in the papers that the real build-up, the alimentation came. Louie, after a week or two on the diet, discovered that she had got a point of view, and not only a point of view but the right one. Not only did she bask in the warmth and inclusion but every morning and evening she was praised. Even the Russians were apparently not as dissatisfied with her as she had feared; there was Stalingrad going on hold-

ing out, but here was she in the forefront of the industrial war drive. As for the Americans now in London, they were stupefied by admiration for her character. Dark and rare were the days when she failed to find on the inside page of her paper an address to or else account of herself. Was she not a worker, a soldier's lonely wife, a war orphan, a pedestrian, a Londoner, a home- and animal-lover, a thinking democrat, a movie-goer, a woman of Britain, a letter writer, a fuel-saver, and a housewife?[10]

Bowen's satiric take on the credulity of the British reading public highlights the way in which the barrier between private and public was breached continually in the creation of wartime myths of identity. The press sought to elevate the individual experience of war to the level of an epic adventure, so that stories of individual disasters or triumphs were absorbed into a communal mythology and the personal narrative threaded into the general ideologically-maintained fabric.

This was particularly the case with regard to the representation of the population as a united front during the Blitz. As bombs fell on Britain's major cities, newspaper headlines prioritised the idea of the ordinary citizen caught up in everyday experiences of triumph over disaster or heroism in the face of danger. In the *Daily Mirror*, for example, a photograph of a man searching the rubble of his destroyed home for his family was coupled with the text: 'The Searcher: Disaster strikes at ordinary folk – and always it forges superb devotion… in man, in woman, in child.'[11] When Buckingham Palace was damaged in 1940, the Queen used the occasion to celebrate the resilience of her most ordinary citizens, announcing 'I'm glad we've been bombed. It makes me feel I can look the East End in the face.' The war was portrayed on a level which involved and concerned the ordinary British family, coping with deprivation, digging for victory in their back gardens and allotments, supporting 'our boys' overseas and smiling in the face of despair. Quite programmatically, the press enabled the Second World War to become the 'People's War', a communal myth which would be sustained in the public imagination for many decades after the end of hostilities.

While such narratives were designed primarily to foster a patriotic consensus at a time of national emergency, they also served to displace or obscure individual experiences of the war in favour of a cohesive public representation. And the versions which media and popular culture sources cultivated were highly resilient, as John Taylor suggests in his study of wartime photography. Commenting on the style and impact of press and cinematic images of war, he emphasises the durability of the collective mythology which emerged from this period:

> Against revision and all political change, the mythic and popular versions of the war remain intact. The mythic history has advantages. It is uncomplicated by detail, and is therefore easy to grasp. As a public memory, it is given solid form in institutions such as museums. It circulates in folklore, in the scripts of newsreels, in films, books and (more recently) in television narrations. The myth is beyond the reach of academic historians. This fabulous history is not just immune, but active; it is able to scoop up disaster and turn it into the stuff of *Boys' Own* heroics.[12]

There was perhaps no more powerful vehicle, in this respect, than British cinema. Since the early 1930s the value of film as a medium for propaganda and the projection of a 'national personality' throughout the Empire had been recognised by the government, and channelled into the work of the Empire Marketing Board and subsequently the National Film Unit, which was set up in 1938.[13] It was largely the films produced by commercial studios such as Rank and Ealing, however, which established a collective narrative of British wartime experience in the aftermath of the war itself. The national stereotypes propagated and perpetuated by commercial cinema are well known, consisting for the most part of British heroism, patriotism and strength of character set against the duplicity and facelessness of Germany or Japan. But once again, cinema focussed on ordinary people bound up in the collective experience. This might be through their efforts on the home front, as in the film *Fires Were Started* (1942), for example, which told of London firefighters during the Blitz, or in battle, with the navy depicted in films such as *In Which We Serve* (1942) and *The Cruel Sea* (1952), and the airforce in *The Battle of Britain* (1959). Repeatedly, cinema drew on the prisoner-of-war experience as a showcase for British integrity and ingenuity, in the 1950 classic, *The Wooden Horse* (1950), *The Colditz Story* (1955), and *Bridge Over the River Kwai* (1957). Women were also addressed through films such as *Carve Her Name With Pride* (1958), which told the true story of the the secret agent Violette Szabo, or *A Town Like Alice* (1956), which portrayed a women's prison camp in Malaysia.[14]

Cinema provided extraordinarily evocative images of the individual at war, cutting across class, gender and regional boundaries in the attempt to portray a collective British interest. While appearing to cover different events and circumstances, it created a unifying image of a small but proud nation, which would win the war not through the might of industrial prowess and military technology, but through individual strength of mind, devotion to duty, and heroic self-sacrifice. What emerges with the success of post-war British cinema is a situation in which 'real' memory is both supplemented and then supplanted by celluloid memory, and in which individual accounts of the war merge with and are conditioned by the narrative produced by film. To an extent therefore the emergence of mass culture, of which cinema is a key component, served to create the version of the war which lodged most securely in the public imagination, and which became, crucially, the version adopted by the present generation as the dominant narrative.

The interruption of private memory by the massed forces of a collectivised narrative is part of a transitional process which Pierre Nora has described in *Les Lieux de Mémoire*. In peasant culture, memories were part of a traditional folkloric repository, but with the advent of mass culture which absorbs the archival role of family, church and school, memories become the documented property of institutions; of newspapers and newsreel, of government records, of museum archives and the cinema. The difference, of course, between private and public resource, is that the latter may serve a particular social or political function. Where private memories select from the past subjectively and at random, public recollection is a process of organisation, management and strategy, geared towards contemporary needs. Once institutionalised, memory can be shaped, adapted, controlled, and if necessary, subdued. As Nora explains, we move from memory as something which is personal in value to history, which is socially constructed and oriented towards the present, an instrument of reconfiguration rather than reclamation.[15] Memory is elided with 'History', providing an authoritative reading of the past arranged in collective and national terms. For the first half of this paper I have explored the way in which a dominant 'narrative of remembrance' was produced through media and popular culture during and after the Second World War. I now wish to turn to the reconfiguration of that narrative within the context of British political culture, first, in the 1950s, and secondly in the 1990s.

There can be little doubt that Britain's internalised wartime self-image helped to sustain the country through the difficulties of the 1950s, and that the memory of the wartime spirit was actively exploited during that period by political and economic strategists. Historians continue to wrangle over the decade, some characterising it as as a highly successful period of cohesive social reform, others lamenting the swift souring of the post-war dream and the cataclysmic mismanagement of social resources.[16] Whatever the case, it is clear that the 1950s were marked by a degree of confusion and insecurity in Britain. If 1945 was the year in which Clement Atlee's Labour government came to power and began to construct the long-promised welfare state, it was also the year which signalled the end of empire, a diminished world status and the prospect of severe economic decline. British society had changed dramatically as a result of the war, in its class and gender relations, in work patterns, in family structures and lifestyle. Traditional values were under strain, the economy and the government were under pressure.

Clearly, the peace was going to be difficult therefore, and so the 'memory' of war became intensely important as a prop to state plans for reform. The dominant narrative suggested that 1945 should be seen not as the end of the war but as a major turning point in British history as a whole and an upturn in the fortunes of British society in particular. If a national depression was to occur, it had to be countered by a continuation of the spirit of the Blitz and the psychological extension of the 1945 victory celebrations, sustained by the idea that Britain had won a 'good' war. As the historian Angus Calder puts it, '[T]hose whose individual wars had not been so 'good' were under some pressure to submerge their traumas and grievances in the national mood of self-congratulation.'[17] Now that they had won a military victory, British citizens were encouraged to pull together to achieve a social victory, and to remember that they had fought for a better world for each other.

As part of this process, the narratives of wartime were continued long beyond the end of the war itself, and the memories of wartime experience were strategically engaged in the battle of post-war social and urban reconstruction. Through invoking the same impulses towards collectivity and consensus, it was possible for the government to manage the difficult transition to peacetime solidarity and state socialism. The euphemistic and relentlessly positive language of wartime propaganda was therefore implemented in relation to domestic policy, with the bulldozing of bombed streets described, for example, as 'necessary slum clearance'. The wartime rhetoric of Winston Churchill, which had sustained the nation in its darkest hour, was now adapted to the concept of 'winning the peace', in order to engage the battle-sentiments of the population in the programme of social reform. Lord Beveridge, the architect of the new welfare initiative, spoke of his hope that the 'principle of service' in the British nation which had enabled it to triumph over the evils of war would now enable it to triumph over the evils of peace, or 'the giants of Want, Disease, Ignorance, Squalor and Idleness.'[18] And it is this spirit, buoyed up by the official narrative of the war and by a public rather than private memory of the experience, which emerges as late as 1965, in the famous concluding paragraph of historian A.J.P. Taylor's *English History, 1914-1945*:

> The British were the only people who went through both world wars from beginning to end. Yet they remained a peaceful and civilised people, tolerant, patient and generous. Traditional values lost much of their force. Other values took their place. Imperialism was on the way out; the welfare state was on the way in. The British Empire declined; the condition of the people improved. Few now sang 'Land of Hope and Glory'. Few even sang 'England Arise'. England had arisen all the same.[19]

In the 1950s therefore, a particular narrative of remembrance was systematically engaged in the creation of a consensus as a basis for the government's economic and welfare policies. But as Britain continued to modernise, and as the idea of British nationhood became increasingly fragmented both culturally and economically, the wartime images of cohesion and community were no longer tenable. Nor did they necessarily fit with subsequent political ideologies, as was illustrated by Margaret Thatcher's tendency to look back to the war not for images of a society 'pulling together' but for those of

British individuality and strong leadership. Thatcher's self-conscious attempts to echo the speeches and indeed political personality of Winston Churchill in her prime-ministerial rhetoric put a very different political complexion on public memory. Allusions to Churchill, the stalwart and ultimately triumphant defender of an assailed nation, reinforced Thatcher's appeal to notions of British independence in the face of intense pressure towards European integration, and provided her with an imagined precedent for 'bulldog' leadership.[20]

Where Thatcher strategically 'remembered' Churchill in the 1980s, the VE Day anniversary celebrations of 1995 similarly drew upon memories of the spirit of the Blitz. The memorial events of that year were a very clear illustration of the way in which public recollection can be superimposed upon private experiences. What is significant is the extent to which the festivities were built up around ideas of re-enactment and reconstruction; the simulation, in short, of the jubilant atmosphere and popular euphoria which Noel Coward describes in his diary entry for the 9th of May 1945:

> Went wandering through the crowds in the hot sunshine. Everyone was good-humoured and cheerful. In the afternoon the Prime Minister made a magnificent speech, simple and without boastfulness, but full of deep pride. In the evening I went along to the theatre and had a drink with the company… We listened to the King's broadcast, then to Eisenhower, Monty and Alexander. Then I walked down the Mall and stood outside Buckingham Palace, which was floodlit. The crowd was stupendous. The King and Queen came out on the balcony, looking enchanting. We all roared ourselves hoarse. …I suppose this is the greatest day in our history.[21]

A glance at the *Daily Telegraph* for the 9th of May, 1995 shows how closely the anniversary celebrations attempted to follow the 'narrative' of 1945. Several pages are devoted to descriptions of the firework displays, concerts, street-parties and other events which marked the day, but throughout there is an emphasis on the re-staging of events and the re-appropriation of a wartime culture. The Buckingham Palace balcony scene was re-created with members of the Royal family appearing before the cheering public. The actor Robert Hardy recited the words with which Winston Churchill had greeted the crowds fifty years earlier, celebrating 'the independent resolve of the British nation', and the singer Vera Lynn, who had been the darling of the British forces during the war, led the throng singing 'There'll be Bluebirds Over the White Cliffs of Dover'. The *Telegraph* reports that the Spitfire which was to have flown over the Palace developed engine trouble, but that a Lancaster Bomber made a triumphant roar past. Local celebrations throughout the country followed similar routines of re-enactment and song. In one village, we are told, locals were forced to relive the crisis of the Blitz when the marquee erected for their VE Day celebrations was burned down by arsonists, but fortunately the plucky villagers, recalling how they had rebuilt their parish church in 1940 after it had been hit by a German bomb, set about cheerfully to repair the damaged tent.

The celebrations were characterised therefore by theatre and spectacle: this was by no means a Wordsworthian process of recollection in tranquillity, but a frenzy of imitation and simulation, with many of the festivities designed not simply to commemorate but to *mimic* the events and emotions of VE Day. Overwhelmingly, the mass experience of the anniversary was one of superficial festivity. The particular 'narrative of memory' which fuelled the popular imagination prioritised victory rather than slaughter, and substituted short-term celebration for any detailed analysis of Britain's long-term post-war legacies, in a kind of selective amnesia. While the rota of VE Day re-enactments served to incorporate within a communal idea of Britishness those who had not been directly involved in the war, they also worked to displace the variant and perhaps even dissenting memories of those who had. Individuals' stories and 'ordinary' experiences were largely contained within the context of a dominant narrative of national solidarity and exultation.

The scale of the carnival and the simulated euphoria which it induced were a means, furthermore, of distracting public attention briefly from Britain's various political and economic problems. In taking a key role in the spectacle, the beleaguered Prime Minister John Major was able to associate himself with the popularity of his wartime predecessor, drawing once again on the image of Churchill in order to reinforce Britain's 'stand-alone' mentality, in opposition to European integration and what many members of the Conservative cabinet regarded as the German economic menace. And inevitably, the management of the festivities gave a welcome boost to the

British Royal family. Beset by scandal, divorce, declining popularity and poor public image, the high visibility of the Royals at the 1995 VE Day anniversary celebrations helped to reinstate them as the family which had led the nation through the trauma of war. The intense media focus on the frail, indomitable and scandal-free figure of the ninety-five-year-old Queen Mother, who represented for many the ideals of family, duty, and self-sacrifice in wartime Britain, was an effective means of shifting the spotlight from the stained reputations of those post-war Royals who had become associated with family break-up, irresponsibility and self-indulgence.

I do not ascribe a systematic or pernicious intentionality to this process of distraction, and in referring to the celebrations as 'simulated', I do not wish to suggest that the emotions expressed by those who participated were in any way artificial. The process of commemoration is a valid one in any society, and in Britain it forms part of a culture which maintains a deep respect for the past. But any dissenting voice is further discouraged by the idea that it is somehow churlish to attack what appeared as a genuinely *popular* celebration. Who would undermine the spirit of VE Day by querying the amount of public money being channelled into fireworks, flypasts and photograph opportunities? Who would grumble about the sale of souvenir mugs, commemorative tea-bags and Union Jack T-shirts? For a brief but meaningful period, Britain was once again the sceptered isle, set in a silver sea.

What emerges from the events of 1995 is a sense that the sheer momentum of the celebrations and the narrative which they endorsed was sufficiently powerful to swamp alternative perspectives. Of course, the anniversary provoked a series of challenges and resistance to the authority of the victory narrative. At one level, dissenting voices were channelled into academic or theoretical discussions in television documentaries, university conferences and journalistic exchanges throughout 1995. At another, they emerged in response to aspects of the commemoration of the war, most notably in the public anger roused in 1992 by plans for the Queen Mother to unveil a statue of Air Chief Marshal Sir Arthur Harris, the man responsible for the 'area bombardment' strategy which enabled British forces to devastate Hamburg, Dresden and several other German cities.[22] It was apparent too, that the frenzy of the VE Day anniversary celebrations in London was not matched by those in Scotland, which tended more towards subdued and reflective church services, or in Northern Ireland where tellingly, very few events were staged. The national consensus which images of the celebrations projected was a fiction which offered a very thin gloss over the underlying regional and social fractures of the United Kingdom

Nonetheless, the narrative of Britain's wartime role has survived, and the nostalgic myth of a 'good war' has undoubtedly contributed to a certain national complacency with respect to what 1945 and its aftermath represented. As many critics have observed, the Second World War did not give rise to the wealth of literature which resulted from the Great War of 1914-18, and has not received the kind of interest which contemporary novelists such as Sebastian Faulks and Pat Barker have developed in its predecessor.[23] In general terms, the Second World War has not been subjected to the same degree of historical revisionism as the First. As a result, its narrative remains comparatively intact and its 'memory' susceptible to exploitation, as has been evident since the VE Day anniversary in the alacrity with which the British tabloid press has employed both wartime stereotypes and anti-German rhetoric in response first, to the European Union ban on contaminated British beef, and secondly to Germany's footballing victory over England in the 1996 European Cup. The fact that such material may be used as burlesque does not detract from the idea that the memory of the Second World War is still relevant to contemporary culture and ideas of nationality, and still vulnerable to contemporary political and journalistic expediency.

The tension between private memory and public recollection which was created by the crisis of the outbreak of war in 1939 has not therefore, been resolved. Rather, one might say, the distance between the two has been stretched further by the demands of the present, and by the dialectic between representation and reality which has emerged alongside the operations of mass media and popular culture. The questions which are now being raised in relation to concepts of Britain and British identity must take into account therefore, the discrepancies between those narratives of remembrance which have been prioritised within the public domain, and the 'unauthorised' versions of the past which remain obscured and perhaps at odds with official histories. They must recognise that memory can be both active and passive, politicised and neutral, complicit and innocent, within the context of the narratives of nation. And finally, they should observe as Pierre Nora has done, the dramatic extent to which our past can become lost in the subtle but crucial slippages between Memory and History:

> Just as the future (formerly a visible, predictable, manipulable, well-marked extension of the present) has come to seem invisible, unpredictable, uncontrollable, so have we gone from the idea of a visible past to an invisible one; from a solid and steady past to our fractured past; from a history sought in the continuity of memory to a memory cast in the discontinuity of history. We speak no longer of 'origins' but of 'births'. Given to us as radically other, the past has become a world apart. Ironically, modern memory reveals itself most genuinely when it shows how far we have come away from it.[24]

Notes

1. Ernest Renan, 'What is a Nation?' (Lecture delivered at the Sorbonne, 11 March 1882), reprinted in Homi Bhabha, ed. *Nation and Narration* (London: Routledge, 1990), trans. Martin Thom, p. 19.
2. See Benedict Anderson, *Imagined Communities: Reflections on the Origin and Spread of Nationalism* (London: Verso, 1991); Homi Bhabha, ed. *Nation and Narration* (London: Routledge, 1990), and Joep Leerssen, *Remembrance and Imagination: Patterns in the Historical and Literary Representation of Ireland in the Nineteenth Century* (Cork: Cork UP and Field Day, 1996).
3. Raphael Samuel, *Theatres of Memory*, 2 vols. (London: Verso, 1994, 1998).
4. For a valuable Lacanian analysis of the distinction, see Michel de Certeau's *The Writing of History* (New York: Columbia UP, 1988), trans. from the French by Tom Conley.
5. Ernest Renan, 'What is a Nation?', p. 11.
6. Alan Bennett, 'The Treachery of Books', *Writing Home* (London: Faber, 1994), p. 3.
7. John Boorman, dir. 'Hope and Glory' (Columbia: Tristar, 1987).
8. For a detailed discussion of First World War narrativisation see Paul Fussell, *The Great War and Modern Memory* (Oxford: Oxford UP, 1975).
9. Raphael Samuel, 'Past and Present in Contemporary Culture', *Theatres of Memory*, vol 1; p. 219.
10. Elizabeth Bowen, *The Heat of the Day* (1948, London: Penguin, 1976), p. 152.

11. For reproductions of press photographs during the war see John Taylor, *War Photography: Realism in the British Press* (London: Routledge, 1991).
12. *War Photography*, p. 56.
13. See James Curran and Vincent Porter, eds., *British Cinema History* (London: Wiedenfield and Nicolson, 1983), ch. 14.
14. See accounts in Anthony Aldgate and Jeffrey Richards, *Britain can take it: the British Cinema in the Second World War* (Edinburgh: Edinburgh UP, 1994), and Philip Taylor, ed., *Britain and the Cinema during the Second World War* (Basingstoke: Macmillan, 1988).
15. 'Between Memory and History: *Les Lieux de Mémoire*', trans. Marc Roudebush, in *Representations* 26 (Spring, 1989), pp. 7-25. This article is a useful summary of Nora's seven volume collaborative work *Les Lieux de Mémoire*, published in Paris between 1984 and 1993.
16. Compare for example, the positive account offered by Peter Hennessy *in Never Again: Britain 1945-51* (London: Cape, 1992), with the more negative reading of Corelli Barnett in *The Lost Victory: British Dreams, British Realities 1945-1950* (London: Macmillan, 1995).
17. Angus Calder, 'Britain's good war?', *History Today* (May, 1995), p. 55.
18. W. H. Beveridge, *Report on Social Insurance and the Allied Services made to His Majesty's Government* (November, 1942).
19. *English History 1914-1945* (Oxford: Clarendon Press, 1965).
20. In a 1977 speech condemning the financial crisis brought about by socialist policy, Margaret Thatcher recalled the solid and spirited Britain of the war years as a prelude to her parody of Churchill's famous speech following the Battle of Britain, in which she simply truncated the phrase 'Never in the field of human conflict was so much owed by so many to so few' to 'Never. ...was so much owed.' See Hans-Jurgen Diller, 'Thatcher in Bruges: A Study in Euro-Rhetoric', *Journal for the Study of British Cultures* vol. 1, no. 2 (1994), pp. 93-109.
21. *Noel Coward Diaries* (London: Wiedenfield and Nicolson, 1982).
22. See Patrick Wright, 'Statues of Liberty', *The Guardian* (1st May,1995) pp. 3-4, in which the author analyses the problematic aspects of public commemoration of war 'heroes'.
23. Paul Fussell is one of many critics who examines the literary impact of the Second World War in *Wartime: Understanding and Behaviour in the Second World War* (Oxford: Oxford UP, 1989). See Sebastian Faulks *Birdsong* (London: Hutchinson, 1993) and Pat Barker's *Regeneration* (London: Viking, 1991) as examples of historical fiction based on the experience of the Great War.
24. Pierre Nora, 'Between Memory and History', pp. 16-17.

Remembering the Great War

Nils Arne Sørensen

In the prologue of Reginald Hill's 1996 detective-novel, *The Wood Beyond*, we find detective sergeant Edgar Wield driving to work through the Yorkshire countryside. On his way, he meets the sheep-farmer George Creed, who is shepherding a flock of sheep into holding pens getting them ready to be sent off. Creed confides that it bothers him to send the sheep off, but "folk have got to eat, that's what farming's all about". He takes comfort in the fact that he has sold his flock to a firm, Haig's, that "give me top price" and furthermore "they'll see them right". After this piece of peasant wisdom, Wield drives on and a few miles later passes the livestock transporter en route for Creed's sheep:

> Wield waved as the huge truck with its legend *D. HAIG & CO Livestock Wholesalers* rumbled by.

Gone are the sheep and Wield continues on his way, now contemplating the weather (Hill, 1996, pp. 1ff.). To a non-British reader, this is a somewhat puzzling way to begin a mystery. However, most British would see it differently. Creed's sheep being picked up by *D. HAIG & CO* translates into a metaphor for World War I, when thousands of young men under the command of Douglas Haig were killed on the Western Front – being led like "lambs to the slaughter". We would therefore expect World War I to play a central role in the novel, and we are not disappointed. Hill's novel is an example that, after 80 years, the Great War still holds a central role in British culture and memory or, to quote the editorial of *The Guardian* on Armistice Day, 1998, "how the leaves of collective memory of the Great War become greener with the passing years".

Not only are the leaves becoming greener. They have also multiplied in recent years. In literature, we have seen the publication of highly acclaimed novels in which the war plays a central role: Pat Barker's *Regeneration Trilogy* (1991-1995), Sebastian Faulks' *Birdsong* (1993), and Helen Dunmore's *Zennor in Darkness* (1993). Geoff Dyer's reflections on the impact of the war on his generation (Dyer was born in 1958) in *The Missing of the Somme* (1994), which combines autobiography, literary analysis and travelogue, is another fascinating example. In 1996, the 80th anniversary of the Battle of the Somme was naturally commemorated, not only at the memorial to the "Missing of the Somme" at Thiepval, but also in the media, where historians and other commentators once again discussed the battle and its legacy. The BBC helped keeping public interest high by producing a major documentary series on the war in 1996. 1997 and 1998 also offered anniversaries, eagerly taken up by the media in articles, books and television documentaries on Passchendaele, the Armistice and the war as such. Thus, the autumn of 1998 saw the publication of books such as John Keegan's eminently readable military history of the war (Keegan, 1998) and Niall Ferguson's iconoclastic *The Pity of War*, both of which were aimed at "the general reader". The BBC produced yet another documentary, *Tommies*, as a tie-in with Armistice Day. As a final example one can mention the campaign to have the 306 British soldiers executed during the war posthumously pardoned. Even if the Labour Government would not grant this, the Army minister John Reid expressed a "deep sense of regret" and urged that the 306 names should be added to their local war memorials (cf. White, 1998).

In this article my aim is not to explain this ongoing interest in the Great War. Instead, I will discuss four key *loci* in the British commemoration of the war as this was shaped during and after the war. *First*, the places of remembrance, that is the war memorials erected all over the country during the post-war years. *Second*, the time of remembrance, that is the establishment and development of Armistice Day as the central moment for reflection on the war. *Third*, the voyages of remembrance, that is the organised travels – or *pilgrimages* – to the battlefields and war cemeteries in the late 1920s. *Fourth*, the literature of remembrance, that is the war books that from the late 1920s were crucial in cementing the canonical reading of the war that has been dominant ever since.

Although commemoration of war was by no means a novelty in Western and British culture, both the forms and scales seen after World War I set new standards. This is easily explicable by the fact that the war itself set new standards. What was soon called the Great War was the first People's War. The outbreak of war was generally met with reactions ranging from stoic patriotism to enthusiasm. During the first 18 months of the war, 2.5 m. British men volunteered – to which should be added 1.7 m. from the Empire. It was only in February 1916 that the Government were forced to introduce conscription. That the support for war was not restricted to men has recently been documented by Angela Woollacott's analysis of female munitions workers. Contrary to the widely held feminist view that women were ill at ease producing agents of death, she convincingly argues that the munitions workers enjoyed both their high wages, their increased freedom – *and producing shells that would kill Germans* (Woollacott, 1995, pp. 194 f.). This fact that the war was fought by the British people, not a professional army, meant that the war would have to be remembered in new ways.

In Britain as elsewhere, the question of the origins of the war have sealed the fate of many a tree over the last 80 years. Today, the dominant orthodoxy is that the British government felt obliged to participate in the war, partly due to obligations to France: partly (and primarily) because of an understanding among governing élites that changes in the European balance of power would inevitably be against Britain's interest (Reynolds, 1991, pp. 89ff; Wilson, 1995). This, however, is far from how the case for war was presented to the public at the time. Here "poor, little Belgium" and the ugly face of German or Prussian militarism were dominant themes[1]. Thus from the very start the war was seen not only as a war for "God, King and Country", but also for Freedom and Justice. To this was added, later on, the ideal of democracy and the vision that this was "the war to end wars". To the British public the war was, in short, presented as "the Great War for Civilisation", to quote the legend on the official victory medal from 1919. This, in Paul Fussell's term (1975), "high diction" understanding of the war naturally played a central role in later rituals of remembrance.

The war that the patriotic soldiers came to experience was very far from the adventurous and glorious scenes presented in boys' magazines and newspaper reports on the campaigns in the colonies. The First World War was the first industrial war in Europe. Heavy artillery, machine-guns and mass armies were the main ingredients. The war not only lasted much longer than expected. It was also much bloodier. More than 1 million men from the British Empire were killed and an even higher number returned from the war as invalids.

Faced with the massive scale of killing, the British authorities decided early on that all soldiers should be buried where they fell. The logistics made it plainly impossible to bring the bodies back to Britain. However, all graves in the war zones were registered, and during the war preparations were mounted for a large scale programme of building war cemeteries. The establishment of the cemeteries began in 1919 under the auspices of the Imperial War Graves Commission. The task was tremendous. Altogether, the commission buried almost 600,000 bodies from the Empire while more than half a million were commemorated on Memorials to the Missing. The war cemeteries were strictly egalitarian. All headstones were alike, and the only individual touch was a short inscription on each stone, according to the wishes of relatives. This egalitarianism was intentional. It stressed the popular or even democratic character of the war. The government would not accept that this was being undermined by wealthy relatives wishing to bring their lost ones back for burial[2].

The decision to erect war cemeteries by the battlefields had important consequences for the culture of remembrance. *First*, as we shall see later, the cemeteries became objects for remembrance in themselves in the form of "pilgrimages". *Second*, the official policy meant that private and public rituals of remembrance became closely linked. To most people, the decision made the grave, the normal focus for private remembrance, inaccessible. Therefore private grief was linked to the public or even national rituals of remembrance: Armistice Day, The Unknown Soldier, and rituals at local war memorials. Thereby, the rituals of remembrance became an important part in the ongoing construction of national identity. *Third*, this shared focus of private and public commemoration meant that acts and rituals of remembrance concentrated on the dead rather than the survivors.

Monuments of Remembrance

The period from ca. 1880 was generally lucrative for sculptors. All over Europe a "statuomania" – as the French historian Maurice Agulhon (1978) has called it – broke out. National heroes, past and present, were honoured in bronze and marble. Among these heroes were the soldiers of the nation-states, and in Britain War Memorials commemorating the Boer War were erected all over country.

The Boer War Memorials were soon to be overshadowed by memorials of the next war. Already during the war, debates on suitable forms of commemorations started, and in 1919 and 1920 both the Victoria & Albert Museum and the Academy of Art sponsored large exhibitions of monuments in order to inspire the commissioners of a war memorial movement that was afoot all over the country. It has been estimated that altogether 40,000 monuments were erected to commemorate the Great War. A general feature of these memorials was that they reflected the new character of the war as a mass war fought by the people. Two of these monuments stand out in a class of their own: The Cenotaph in Whitehall and the grave of The Unknown Warrior in Westminster Abbey. Their stories are well-known and here a brief summary will do.

The cenotaph was originally a temporary monument, in wood and plaster, designed by Sir Edwin Lutyens. It was erected in connection with the Imperial Victory Parade on July 19, 1919 when it was the centre for the parading troops' salute to the fallen. The form chosen by Lutyuens was ripe with connotations. A cenotaph, that is an empty grave, was both a symbol of the graves away from home and the thousands of missing. At the same time, the empty grave linked the monument to Christian tradition. It also proved immensely popular. On Armistice Day 1919, thousands of people gathered by the cenotaph, which was used as the centre for official commemoration by representatives of the royal family, the government and the military. Thus Empire, God, and private grief could melt together in the monument, and it is not surprising that

Lutyens' wood and plaster monument was given a permanent form in 1920.

The same year saw the entombment of the Unknown Warrior. The idea was put forward by the dean of Westminster Abbey and quickly supported by Lloyd George. The Unknown Warrior was chosen in Flanders by a blindfolded officer from the bodies of six unidentified fallen soldiers. The chosen one was transferred to a coffin of solid *English* oak, sailed to *Dover*, put on a train to *London* and on Armistice Day marched through London accompanied by the military leaders of the war. Finally, he was put to rest in *Westminster Abbey*. Originally, the grave was simply adorned with the legend "An Unknown Soldier", but this was soon changed to the telling inscription that we can still see today:

BENEATH THIS STONE RESTS THE BODY
OF A BRITISH WARRIOR
UNKNOWN BY NAME OR RANK
BROUGHT FROM FRANCE TO LIE AMONG
THE MOST ILLUSTRIOUS OF THE LAND

AND BURIED HERE ON ARMISTICE DAY
11 NOV: 1920, IN THE PRESENCE OF
HIS MAJESTY KING GEORGE V
HIS MINISTERS OF STATE
THE CHIEFS OF HIS FORCES
AND A VAST CONCOURSE OF THE NATION

THUS ARE COMMEMORATED THE MANY
MULTITUDES WHO DURING THE GREAT
WAR OF 1914-1918 GAVE THE MOST THAT
MAN CAN GIVE LIFE ITSELF
FOR GOD
FOR KING AND COUNTRY
FOR LOVED ONES HOME AND EMPIRE
FOR THE SACRED CAUSE OF JUSTICE AND
THE FREEDOM OF THE WORLD

The monument immediately caught the public imagination. More than a million people paid homage by passing the grave in November 1920 (cf. Blythe, 1963, pp. 7-14; Gregory, 1994, pp. 24-26).

The appeal of the Grave can be explained by the fact that the unknown soldier represented the more than 500,000 dead from the British and Imperial forces whom the authorities had not been able to identify. The Grave also stressed the popular and democratic character of the war: The unknown man of the people was laid to rest among *the most illustrious of the nation*.

Much less is known about the rest of the monuments. Most war memorials have been dismissed by art historians as "monuments of low grade architectural quality and banality of inspiration" (Assunto, 1965, p. 291). It is only in recent years that the war memorials have caught the attention of historians. The pioneers in this field have been Reinart Koselleck (1979) Antoine Prost (1984, 1986), George Mosse (1990), and Ken Inglis (1992a, 1992b, 1993). More recently Jay Winter (1995) has added to our understanding. Although our knowledge is still fragmentary, some overall patterns can be pointed to. The ubiquity of the monuments is the first thing that springs to mind. Every town and village has local monuments. To this should be added monuments in work-places, in churches, in clubs, in schools and universities, and, of course, the military monuments. Extreme examples of this commemoration craze are found in Meriden Green where a memorial is erected to "the lasting memory of those cyclists who died in the Great War" and in Lake on the Isle of Wight a memorial remembers "the horses and dogs who also bore the burden and heat" (cf. Boorman, 1988, p. 2; Borg, 1991, pp. 90-91).

If we look into the origins of the memorials, they seem typically to have sprung from local initiatives. Normally headed by local grandees, committees started collecting funds for a memorial, and typically also decided on the form of the memorial, albeit often after some public debate.

As a example to illustrate this, I have chosen a work-place monument, the war memorial of the Public Record Office (PRO). The history of this can, not surprisingly, be traced in detail in the records of the PRO[3]. In a meeting of the Departmental Council on October 22, 1920, it was agreed "that a memorial to those of the Public Record Office who had fallen during the recent war, was a desirable thing". To this end, a War Memorial Committee was set up. In its first meeting in November 1920, this committee decided that such a monu-

The war memorial of Landown in the Isle of Wight, situated on the sea-side promenade. The memorial is inspired by Reginald Blomfield's Cross of Remembrance used in the British war cemeteries.

ment should have the form of a stone tablet and be placed in the museum of the archive. The committee also

> propose[d] to concentrate on a Memorial to the Dead, and possibly, if some small funds are left over, to print for distribution to those concerned, and for preservation by the Office, a Roll of Service similar to those which have been framed in the Entrance Halls

Over the next year, the committee organised a subscription of funds for the monument, decided on the precise format and negotiated contracts with architects and a stone mason. Finally, in May 1922, the memorial was unveiled by the Master of the Rolls. From the deliberations of the war memorial committee three things are worth mentioning. *First*, the form of the memorial. The committee decided on a traditional artistic form. *Second*, the location of the memorial. This was chosen to be not only in the museum, but the committee also wanted it situated in the most prestigious place in the museum. A letter from the committee, dated February 1921, stated:

> [T]he site in the Museum should be that selected independently by the Architect and by this Committee and generally regarded as the most important and the best place there; namely, the space between the Young and Bruce Monuments.

Third, there seems to have been a telling change during the planning process as to whom to commemorate. That it should be a memorial to the dead was clear from the beginning, but the dead were originally strongly linked to the much larger group of PRO employees who had served in the war. In its first meeting in November 1920, the war memorial committee contemplated using possible left over funds for the making of a roll of service of all who participated in the war. This suggestion was not adopted. It was the dead rather than the living that should be remembered. A parallel can be seen in the inscription discussed by the committee. The original proposal focused almost as much on the fact that "THIS MEMORIAL was erected by the other Members of the Staff" as on the objective of the memorial to commemorate "[the] MEMORY of the following Members of the Public Record Office who died on Service during the War [followed by a list of names]". However, this was later changed into a brief "Erected by their colleagues". A comment from the Departmental Whitley Council, under whose authority the war memorial committee worked, furthermore stressed that "[t]he words 'Erected by their colleagues' should be in appreciably smaller type than the rest of the inscription."

In all of this, the PRO memorial resembles what we find elsewhere. Typically, traditional artistic forms were chosen. To the chagrin of art connoisseurs but easily explicable: the committees wanted to erect lasting memorials and therefore naturally adopted well known forms such as obelisks, crosses, columns, cenotaphs, and arches. The exception to this rule is the many memorials which consist of statues of Tommies – the average, common soldier – stressing the popular character of the war. It is also typical that memorials were placed in central positions. Typically in the main town square or in front of the village church. That the war memorial in the seaside resort Landown is situated on the beach is in this sense perfectly logical. Finally, in the memorials the dead were typically the centre of attention. That this was not a given thing is demonstrated by the PRO example, and according to Ken Inglis ca. 5% of the British war memorials actually commemorates the people who *served*, not necessarily died, in the war. However, although this is significant compared to other European countries, it still leaves 95% of the monuments to be exclusively memorials to the fallen. The PRO inscription also falls in line with the general pattern in being brief and to the point. More importantly, the central inscription is actually the names of the fallen, another common feature. Not only were the names listed; they were listed alphabetically, thus stressing the democratic character of the war and the sacrifice offered.

In the post-war years the war memorials were used in both the private, the semi-public and the public culture of commemoration. Typically, the members of the local branches of the veteran organisation, The British Legion, included a ceremony at the local memorial as part of their annual meeting. However, it was primarily in the ceremonies of Armistice Day, the Day of Remembrance, that people gathered by the memorials.

Time of Remembrance

The news of the Armistice of November 11 1918 was greeted with jubilation in Britain. In London, the wealthy partied at the Ritz and the poor danced in the streets of East End. According to A.J.P. Taylor (1965, pp. 156 f.), celebrations went far beyond dancing and "ran on with increasing wildness for three days, when the police finally intervened and restored order". This was hardly an ideal on which to build an official tradition of remembrance, and it is not in the aftermath of the 1918 celebrations that we find the roots of what became the key national rituals of commemoration.

As Adrian Gregory has shown in his both thorough and excellent analysis of Armistice Day (1994), the idea to turn Armistice Day into a Day of Remembrance was first launched by the former high commissioner for South Africa, Sir Percy Fitzpatrick, in early November 1919. In a memorandum to the government he suggested the introduction of a short silence on Armistice Day to "remember and salute the fallen." Both the government and the King supported the idea, and on November 7 the newspapers printed a personal request from the King to respect "for the brief space of two minutes a complete suspension of all our normal activities" on "the eleventh hour of the eleventh day of the eleventh month." A plethora of evidence – ranging from newspapers to private letters – witness that the two minutes' silence was a great success. That a tradition had been born is evident from the newspaper coverage of Armistice Day in 1920 when the ritual was presented as so well-established that it was not questioned, not even by the socialist *Daily Herald*.

The Silence was not the only ritual of Armistice Day. The royal family used the day to pay homage to the fallen by laying down a wreath at the Cenotaph, and throughout the country, local war memorials became the setting for ceremonies. Speeches by local dignitaries, prayers, sermons and hymns were key ingredients in the national-religious ceremonies. Soon the Sunday closest to November 11 was established as "Remembrance Sunday" with special church services and collections. Also Armistice Day was linked to charity work by the British Legion's "Poppy Appeal". A telling indicator of the popularity of the paper Haig Poppies is that Dorothy Sayers used the poppy as the crucial clue in her *The Unpleasantness at the Bellona Club*, as early as 1928 (cf. Cannadine, 1981, p. 225).

In the early post-war years the legacy of the 1918 celebrations could still be felt. Armistice Day was also a day of society Victory Balls and less formal drunken festivities. This met with growing criticism. In the early 1920s, one can follow a debate between those who wanted Armistice Day to focus on the commemoration of the sacrifice of the dead and those who believed that the day should also celebrate victory (and survival). The result was nicely summed up by the veteran Charles Carrington when he wrote that from the mid-1920s "imperceptibly, the Feast-Day became a Fast Day". According to Carrington, this meant that "many old soldiers" felt left out. Gregory convincingly sees this as a marginalisation of the veterans and their role. It was not the memories and contribution of the survivors, but the sacrifice of the fallen and the grief of the bereaved that were central in the Armistice Day rituals (cf. Gregory, 1994, pp. 51-92).

The only dissenting voices were from the left. Throughout the 1920s, *The Daily Herald* insisted on remembering the living. According to their analysis, the heroes of the war had become the victims of the post-war economic recession. The unemployment queues were compared in dramatic fashion to the endless rows of crosses in the war cemeteries. But the socialists failed to force unemployment problems on to the central agenda of Armistice Day. They did, however, play a role in another clear trend of change in the contents and meaning of Remembrance Day. From the late 20s, speeches and articles surrounding Armistice Day focused more and more clearly on a reading of the Great War as "the war to end wars".

That this was an illusion hardly needs to be restated. One of the victims of this illusion was Armistice Day and the Great Silence. Both were given up during World War II, and in 1946 Remembrance Sunday took over the role as the national day for commemoration of the dead in Britain's wars.

This cartoon from Daily Herald *on Armistice Day in 1927 with Mars hovering above the ceremony of remembrance at the Cenotaph is a typical example of the leftwing interpretation of the war in the 1920s.*

Voyages of remembrance

That the battle fields where British soldiers had fought and died and the war cemeteries where they were buried would be central places for the commemoration of the war was clear when the war ended. Already in 1919 detailed travel books such as Michelin's guide to *The Marne Battlefields* were published. Grieving relatives (who had the economic means) also started to go to the cemeteries abroad. The central position of the battlefields and the cemeteries in the official commemoration of the war was underlined in 1922 when

> The King went forth on pilgrimage
> His prayers and vows to pay
> To them that saved our heritage
> And cast their own away

to quote the opening lines of Kipling's poem inspired by the journey (Kipling, 1922, p. 668).

Organised travels to the battle fields were discussed by the veteran organisation The British Legion from 1926[4]. A trip planned for legion delegates in the spring of 1926 did not materialise but in 1927 the organisation arranged four tours to Belgium and France to "relive old memories". A lot of energy was put into marketing the tours, especially in *The British Legion Journal*. Thus, in the article "Battlefield Pilgrimage", "One Who Means to Pilgrim" wrote,

> Have you not longed to take the missus and show her the actual spot where you over-the-topped on that first breathless occasion, or the trench, or what remains of it, where you held on against desperate odds. Have you not felt the desire mounting up as the years go on to see the last resting-place of the pal you left behind you, to stand in the silence by his grave, and in so doing refresh your soul for the fulfilment of your resolve that his widow or dependants shall not be left uncared for and unhelped. But want of opportunity, difficulties of language, passport, ways and means, have loomed up too large and prevented realisation. Today, however, you have your chance. Don't miss it! The legion has arranged a comfortable and economical visit to the Mecca of the British Army – the Ypres Salient.
> (*British Legion Journal*, vol. 6, p. 265).

This is a barely hidden advertisement that also tells us of the way the quasi-official British Legion understood the war as a mixture of adventure and male bonding that went beyond death.

The tours took place in June of 1927 and were judged by the Legion to be a success to be repeated the next year. However, the arrangement had not been noticed by the British press. When the American Legion planned to hold its annual delegate meeting in Paris in September 1927 and as part of it arrange travels to the battle fields for 20,000 American war veterans, *The Daily Mail* was quick to suggest a British parallel.

From the material in the archive of the British Legion it seems clear that this media interest caused the Legion to expand its plans for 1928. A circular of November 1927 told of plans for "10,000 Ex-Service Men under the Leadership of their president, field marshal Earl Haig ... [to] return to the Battle Areas which they knew and revisit the scenes of the great Battles". These plans turned into reality in early August 1928 when some 11,000 travelled from Britain and Ireland to Belgium and France where they visited battlefields and war cemeteries. The travellers finally convened in Ypres. Here the tour culminated with a "Remembrance Service" and the legionaries marching past their new president, Admiral Jellicoe, their patron, the Prince of Wales, and military leaders from the allied countries and through the Menin Gate that in 1927 had been inaugurated as memorial for the missing from the Ypres battles.

The tour, officially "British Legion Battlefields Pilgrimage", was a mixture of "trench tourism" and a national-religious pilgrimage to cemeteries and memorials. It was thoroughly documented in the press, and especially in the *British Legion Journal*. In this journal reports stressed the remembrance of fallen comrades but equally that the tours served to revive "that sense of unity and friendliness which existed during the War, and which after the event have somewhat submerged" as one could read in the report in "The Women's Section" of the Legion's journal (vol. 8, p. 69). The newspaper reports also stressed other elements, especially that the tour served as a way to build bridges between the ex-soldiers and their relatives who had experienced the war at home. Finally, for many pilgrims the visit to the cemeteries was the key element where they, often for the first time, had the chance to visit the graves of husbands, fathers, sons and fiancées. The centre of attention in the reporting was, however, the large-scale ceremonies in Ypres on August 8. The event was highly ritualised borrowing from the well-established traditions of

Armistice Day: wreath-laying ceremonies, solemn speeches, singing of hymns, and, of course, the two minutes' silence. National, religious and military elements mixed in the ceremonies which furthermore were presented as a celebration of the victory. And the ceremonies could not only be followed in press reports. The BBC transmitted the service at the Menin Gate. Thus, the battlefield tour was turned into a national event.

Plans to copy the arrangement and develop it further, for instance with trips to Gallipoli, were launched after this success. However, these plans all came to nought. Battlefield Pilgrimages did not establish themselves as a truly national ritual. But tours continued in the following years. Not on a national scale, but as local initiatives by Legion branches. An indication of the scale of this activity can be found in the fact that in 1931 the British Legion established a "Haig House" for "pilgrims" in Ypres.

Even though a large scale annual pilgrimage to the battlefields did not establish itself as a tradition, the 1928 event is telling of the variety of remembrances of the war. Grief, national pride and fond memories of "the good, old days" were the main elements. This has parallels with some of the traditions established around Armistice Day (especially the gatherings in The Royal Albert Hall where veterans met and remembered and sang the songs of the trenches[5]) but is a far cry from the perception of the war that was in the process of being canonised by a new flood of war books from the late 1920s.

Literary Remembrance[6]

In literary terms, the process of remembering the war began before the war started. The outbreak of war resulted in a flood of literature of anticipation, in Britain and elsewhere. Rupert Brooke's "1914 Sonnets" are the most famous and influential British example of anticipated remembrance. The deeply felt patriotism and longing for action and adventure that dominate Brooke's poems remained the central themes in the most literary representations of war during the war. Among such "Monuments to War" (Hynes, 1991) are most of the reports on the war in the press, and popular novels such as Brenda Girvin's *Munition Mary* (1918) and John Buchan's Richard Hannay novels (1915-19). Popular novels from the early post-war period by Wilfred Ewart (1921) and Ernest Raymond (1922) are also in a similar vein although patriotic enthusiasm to some extent had turned into a sense of patriotic duty.

With the exception of Rupert Brooke, none of the authors mentioned so far entered what today is seen as the canon of war books. And Brooke's role in the canon has primarily been that of serving as a counter-point. He has become the incarnation of the pre-war notions of war that were blown to smithereens in the trenches. The actual war experience, on the other hand, was what middle-class soldier-poets such as Robert Graves, Siegfried Sassoon and Wilfred Owen struggled to put into words from the middle period of the war. Central themes in their representation of the war are the actual face of war (death, pain, fear, fatigue), soldiers as a brotherhood, and the gap between the fighting soldiers and the rest of society[7].

However, this new and "realistic" way of rendering the war experience did not establish itself as dominant. While the sales figures of the poetry collections of new war poets like Owen could be counted in hundreds, by the mid-1920s the poems of Brooke had sold some 300,000 copies, and Raymond's *Tell England* had gone into its 22nd printing (cf. Gregson, 1976, p. 8; Ceadel, 1994, p. 239).

This changed in 1928 when "war books" developed into the new fashion with the publication of Edmund Blunden's *Undertones of War*, Sassoon's *Memoirs of a Fox-hunting Man* and R.C. Sheriff's play, *Journey's End*. The trend continued over the following years with books by Richard Alderston, Robert Graves, Frederic Manning, and Vera Brittain whose *Testament of Youth* (1933) presented the war as destruction and loss from a female perspective (cf. Olesen & Sørensen, 1987). Furthermore, books such as A.P. Herbert's *The Secret Battle*, originally published in 1919, became the object of new interest (no less than five editions were published from 1928 to 1936). Finally, we should add Ernest Hemingway's *A Farewell to Arms* and, of course, Erich Maria Remarque's international best-seller *All Quiet on the Western Front*, to complete the picture.

The ambition of these books was summed up by Remarque in his introductory note to *All Quiet on the Western Front* (1928):

> This story is neither an accusation nor a confession and least of all an adventure, for death is not an adventure to those who stand face to face with it. It will try simply to tell of a generation of men who, even though they may have escaped its shells, were destroyed by the war.[8]

All of these authors followed in the foot-steps of the British war poets. They were all war veterans and wanted to tell, whether in memoirs, novels or plays, "wie es eigenlich gewesen ist". Their books dealt with fear and death, mud, lice, drunkenness, sex, inhuman superior officers and the strong bonds between officers and men, the fighters, at the front. By writing about the reality of war, the authors wanted to bridge the gap between fighters and non-fighters, be it those who kept the home fires burning or those who were too young to have participated. Central in many of the books was the portrayal of the war as the decisive experience of a generation, the lost generation who was lost whether they had survived the shells or not, as Remarque put it.

Another characteristic is that most of the books – both memoirs and novels – offer a three stage developmental narrative. Life (and history) is divided into very distinct pre-war, war and post-war eras. Edwardian Britain is seen as a youthful Arcadia, often set in the countryside, dominated by friendship, family, love and the high ideals of patriotism and civilisation/progress. It is these ideals that carry the young generation into the war where they are destroyed in the furnace of modern, industrial warfare. What makes the war experience (just) bearable are the strong bonds developed among the fighters who are portrayed as a caste set apart from both the leaders of the war ("the old men") and society at home in general. To the fighter-authors the war is seen as lost. The high ideals died as they were first betrayed in the endless and useless bloody battles of the war and then later betrayal continued with the harsh peace treaties. Added to this came the politicians' promises of "a land fit for heroes" which simply turned into just empty promises[9].

Finally, one must stress the theme of the lost generation. Not only were one million British soldiers killed; it was the 'best and the brightest' who died, leaving "second rate masculine ability ... [to] ... struggle helpless with almost insoluble problems because the first-rate were gone from a whole generation," to quote Vera Brittain (1933, pp. 259f.).

Samuel Hynes (1991) has summed up all these elements as "the war myth". According to Hynes they came to constitute the dominant reading of the war from ca. 1930. The explanation of the delayed success of this critical reading is not difficult to find. Its precondition was that the post-war period had lasted long enough for central features to have fixed themselves as being characteristics of a distinct "new era".

Economic problems and unemployment queues had, by the late 1920s, demonstrated that the war had not resulted in "a land fit for heroes". Internationally, the weakness of the League of Nations and the rise of dictatorships in the Mediterranean and in Eastern and Central Europe indicated that the Great War had neither been "the war to end wars" nor secured the victory of democracy and freedom. Therefore, the sacrifices of war had been in vain, and it was now much more difficult to give the war a positive meaning.

This is not necessarily the argument of the authors of the war books. To many writers, describing the reality of war as a formative experience for them and their generation seems to have been the main ambition. However, it was the background of growing disillusionment that created the mass market for their books, some of which had proved very difficult to sell less than a decade earlier. To mention just one example, it was only when Owen's poems were published in a new edition in 1931 that he gained his position as a spokesman for the "lost generation", whose poems were seen as monuments of pity for the dead but also as a warning to the living.

Conclusion

If we leave Britain and broaden our perspective to the other participants in the First World War, we find many similarities in the cultures of commemoration. In most countries Armistice Day was ritualised; in some, for example France, it was even turned into a national holiday. We find entombed Unknown Soldiers and National War Memorials all over Europe (and in the United States, Australia, Canada, India, etc.) (Inglis, 1993). With the exception of Russia, where the new Bolshevik rulers saw no reason to commemorate the war, we also find war memorials in towns and villages all over the continent, that is, if they survived the Second World War (or the censorship of first the Nazis, then the Allies, in the case of Germany). The boom in war books from the late 1920s was also an international phenomenon.

This interest was not only found in countries which had participated in the war. Some Danish examples can serve to illustrate this. A wide selection of the war books was quickly translated into Danish. For example, *All Quiet on the Western Front*, in an excellent translation by the author Tom Kristensen, was published in 1929 and printed in 50,000 copies within four months. Denmark also got a National War Memorial, on July 1, 1934, when a "Mindelunden" in Aarhus was unveiled in the presence of the Royal family and some 30,000 spectators. This monument's most original feature is that it depicts the war as fratricide, a result of the dominant anti-militarist mood of the time and the fact that Danes fought and died on both sides of the war. Thus the Danish monument is a striking example of translating the sacrifice of the war into a warning to present and future generations of the futility of war, a reading that was prominent in many countries from the late 1920s.

If we leave out the commemoration (or better: celebration) of the war that we find in the Fascist dictatorships[10], general patterns are evident, and the history of the British culture of remembrance can easily be copied into other national settings.

At least, if we look only at the inter-war period. However, once we follow the memory of the Great War into the second post-war period, the British experience stands in a league of its own. In continental European countries, the First World War became overshadowed by the Second. In Britain, however, the two wars became both intertwined and separated. Intertwined in the sense that after 1945 the promises of 1918 were finally fulfilled. The Labour Government of 1945-1951 did not only promise a land fit for heroes; they actually set forth to build it with impressive welfare legislation.

However, this actually helped to separate the wars and cement the picture of the First World War as futile. The futility of World War One was underlined by the simple fact that the second war had to be fought. The wars were also separated by the quality of the enemy: Kaiser Wilhelm was no match for Hitler. Finally, as early as 1940, the notion of the war as "The People's War" was established. Here we should stress that "people's war" not only indicated an equality of sacrifice between the social classes (to a high degree a myth, as social historians never tire to point out), but also between front and home. Thus, a central and divisive element in the "war myth" was avoided in the Second World War.

These differences were so marked that, after 1945, we find two very different "war myths" at large in British culture. World War Two was firmly established as "Britain's Finest Hour", the courageous struggle for not only democracy and a "British way of life" but for Humanity in general as Churchill often stressed. Compared to this, World War One became the "bad war" and served as the point of reference to war as a civilisation in crisis. This understanding has been inculcated, not so much at war memorials or on Remembrance Sunday, as in schools, literature, films and the media in general. Gallipoli, Somme and Passchendaele have become household metaphors for the folly of men, and Douglas Haig & Co are seen as the cold-blooded slaughterers of innocent lambs.

In recent years, some historians have questioned this dominant understanding of the war. John Fuller (1990) and Joanna Bourke (1996), among others, have given us new insights into troop morale, the relationship between front and home and between officers and men. Military historians have pointed out that Haig's strategy of mass battles actually won the war, however bloody they were. As a consequence of the canonisation of the 'War Myth', other interpretations of the war seem to have been repressed or at least forgotten. There is ample evidence that not everyone subscribed to the bleak picture of the dominant interpretation. The material offered here on the trench tourism of the late 1920s also suggests that far from all those belonging to the war generation felt that they "were destroyed by the war.". Another example are the many short stories, novels and memoirs published in *The British Legion Journal* during the 1920s and 30s; they are closer to the patriotic image of the war than to the war myth[11]. A final indication that both the reality and memory of the war were more complex than generally presented can be taken from the material world of advertising. In 1928 the firm "Armour" advertised its corned beef with positive references to the war years: A picture of a group of smiling Tommies was followed by this text:

"Remember how fit you felt then? When your face was copper-coloured and you glowed with that "push-a-bus-over" feeling. You owed that to corned beef. Well, just try Armour's Veribest Corned Beef to-day."
(*Daily Mail*, August 19, 1928).

Corned beef advertisement 1928.

It is a far cry from tanned Tommies to the broken generation of the war myth. However, the topic under discussion here is not how the war really *was*, but how it was and still is *remembered*. This memory is, of course, a construction, founded on a plethora of different monuments erected ever since 1914. It might well be that we, as professional historians, should deconstruct this memory. In doing so, however, we should be aware that we might very well destroy the Great War as a memory and reduce it to plain history, that is to being simply part of a past with little relevance for the present.

Notes

1. Excellent examples of this can be found in the satirical magazine *Punch*. Cf. *Mr. Punch's History of the Great War* (London: Cassell, 1919), passim.
2. For the history of war cemeteries, see Gibson & Ward, 1989, pp. 43-57.
3. The material relating to the memorial is found in PRO/PRO 39/6: Public Record Office War Memorial.
4. The following is based on the (meagre) holdings of the archive of The Royal British Legion (Haig House, London), *The British Legion Journal* and, for the 1928 Pilgrimage, the coverage in the national newspapers *The Daily Herald*, *The Daily Mail*, *The Manchester Guardian*, and *The Times*.
5. This tradition was turned into a national event by the transmissions of the BBC. It has continued as one of the core rituals of Armistice Day to the present.
6. The literature on the 'war books' and, more generally, the war and the British cultural elites, is vast. I have been primarily inspired by Fussell (1975), Wohl (1979) and Hynes (1991).
7. The same trend can be found in the visual arts in painters as Christopher Nevinson (e.g. his "Paths of Glory", 1917), Paul Nash (e.g. "We are making a new world", 1918) and the sculptor Charles Sargeant Jagger ("No Man's Land", 1919). For an excellent analysis of the war and the fine arts, see Richard Cork, 1994.
8. Quoted from Lewis Milestone's film version of Remarque's novel, released to great critical acclaim in 1930. The film won additional fame because the Nazis reacted violently against it and forced the German government to ban the film in 1930. *All Quiet on the Western Front* was, however far from the only war film being produced in Hollywood and elsewhere from the late 1920s. Other famous examples are W.P. Pabst's *Westfront* (Germany, 1930), James Whale's *Journey's End* (Great Britain, 1930), Frank Borzage's *A Farewell to Arms* (USA, 1932) and Jean Renoir's *La grande illusion* (France, 1937). The mass appeal of film was tremendous in the inter-war years – in 1939, twenty million tickets

were sold in Britain, and in Liverpool, for instance, 40 per cent of the population went to the cinema at least once a week (cf. Mason, 1997, p. 5) – and films like these probably did much more to form public opinion and collective memory about the war than the most successful books. However, there is little doubt that the books informed the opinions of the film makers, and some of the most successful films were adaptations of war books.
9. Although he did not write any 'war books', the works of (war veteran) J.P. Priestley fit nicely into this pattern. The romantic socialist Priestley was obsessed with the divide between pre-1914 and post-1918 England. Before the war, life and society were dominated by English virtues; in the inter-war period materialism, technology, superficiality, in short Americanisation (or modernity) dominated.
    Priestley is a clear example of how the war experience strengthened anti-modernist trends among the cultural elites, and it might be fruitful to examine the impact of the war in order to further explore the cultural roots of the 'Decline of Britain'.
10. This can be illustrated by looking at Italy where the war was not only commemorated but also widely celebrated as the fourth war of unification (which explains why the Unknown Soldier was buried in the *Vittoriale* in Rome, the monument celebrating the unification of Italy). Furthermore, the war was seen as the hour of birth of Fascism itself and of the New Italy that Mussolini wanted to create. Therefore many war memorials in Italy have clearly militarist messages: Here the soldier is still the active hero, and that dying for your country is "dulce et decorum" has not been questioned. After 1945, many of the monuments were given a new meaning by now also commemorating the heroes of the anti-fascist resistance movement; although only in few places authorities went to the lengths seen in Tuscan San Gimignano where the Fascist and militarist monument now sports the legend: "San Gimignano ai suoi caduti in guerra perché tutti ricordino sempre che la pace fa la grandezza dei popoli" [Erected by San Gimignano to its fallen so all will remember that it is peace that makes peoples great]. Thus, the commemoration of war is seen closely linked to the political developments and cultures of Italy (A parallel story can be told about Germany before and after 1933).
11. These texts are analysed in Vinnie Christensen's M.A.-thesis, *Cultural Interpretations of the Great War* (Department of English, Odense University, 1997).

Bibliography

M. Agulhon (1978), 'La Statuomanie et l'Histoire', in *Ethnologie Française*, 3-4.
R. Assunto (1965), 'Monuments, 19th and 20th Centuries', in *Encyclopedia of World Art*, vol. 10, New York.
P. Barker (1991), *Regeneration*, London.

B. Barker (1993), *The Eye in the Door*, London.
P. Barker (1995), *The Ghost Road*, London.
E. Blunden (1928/1937), *Undertones of War*, 3rd ed., Harmondsworth.
R. Blythe (1963), *The Age of Illusion*. England in the Twenties and Thirties, 1919-1940, London.
D. Boorman (1988), *At the Going Down of the Sun*. British First World War Memorials, York.
A. Borg (1991), *War Memorials from Antiquity to the Present*, London.
J. Bourke (1996), *Dismembering the Male*, London.
British Legion Journal, vol. 1-17, 1921-1938.
V. Brittain (1933/1978), *Testament of Youth 1890-1925*, London.
R. Brooke (1914), '1914', in G. Keynes (ed.), *The Poetical Works of Rupert Brooke*, London 1946.
J. Buchan (1915), *The 39 Steps*, London.
J. Buchan (1916), *Freemantle*, London.
J. Buchan (1919), *Mr. Standfast*, London.
B. Bushaway (1992), 'Name upon Name: The Great War and Remembrance', in R. Porter (ed.), *Myths of the English*, Cambridge.
D. Cannadine (1981), 'War and Death, Grief and Mourning in Modern Britain', in J. Whale (ed.), *Mirrors of Mortality*. Studies in the Social History of Death, London 1981.
M. Ceadal (1994), 'Attitudes to War: Pacifism and Collective Security', in P. Johnson (ed.), *Twentieth Century Britain*: Economic, Social and Cultural Change, London.
V. Christensen (1997), *Cultural Interpretations of the Great War*, Odense.
R. Cork (1994), *A Bitter Truth*. Avant-Garde Art and the Great War, New Haven.
H. Dunmore (1993), *Zennor in Darkness*, London.
G. Dyer (1994), *The Missing of the Somme*, London.
W. Ewart (1921), *Way of Revelation*, London.
S. Faulks (1993), *Birdsong*, London.
N. Ferguson (1998), *The Pity of War*. The First World War and the Twentieth Century, London.
J.G. Fuller (1990), *Troop Morale and Popular Culture in the British and Dominion Armies, 1914-1918*, Oxford.
T.A.E. Gibson & G.K. Ward (1989), *Courage Remembered* The story behind the construction and maintenance of the Commonwealth's Military Cemeteries and Memorials of the Wars of 1914-1918 and 1939-1945, London.
B. Girvin (1918), *Munition Mary*, London.
R. Graves (1929/1960), *Goodbye to All That*, rev. ed., Harmondsworth.
A. Gregory (1994), *The Silence of Memory*. Armistice Day 1919-1946, Oxford.
A. P. Herbert (1919/1928), *In Secret Battle*, 3rd. ed., London.
R. Hill (1996), *The Wood Beyond*, London.
S. Hynes (1990), *A War Imagined*. The First World War and English Culture, London.

K. Inglis (1992a), 'War memorials: ten questions for historians', in *Guerres mondiales*, 167/1992.
K. Inglis (1992b), 'The Homecoming: The War Memorial Movement in Cambridge, England', in *Journal of Contemporary History*, 27, 1992.
K. Inglis (1993), 'Entombing Unknown Soldiers: from London and Paris to Baghdad', in *History and Memory*, 5.
J. Keegan (1998), *The First World War*, London.
R. Kipling (1922), "The King's Pilgrimage", in R. Kipling, *The Collected Verse*, London, 1990.
R. Koselleck (1979), 'Kriegerdenkmale as Identitätsstiftungen der Überlebenden', in O. Marquard & K. Stierle (eds.), *Identität*, München.
T.W. Laqueur (1994), 'Memory and Naming in the Great War', in J.R. Gillis (ed.), *Commemorations*. The Politics of National Identity, Princeton.
T. Mason (1997), "'Hunger ... is a Very God Thing': Britain in the 1930s', in N. Tiratsoo (ed.), *From Blitz to Blair*. A New History of Britain since 1939, London.
G. L. Mosse (1990), *Fallen Soldiers*. Reshaping the Memory of the World Wars, Oxford.
T.B. Olesen & N.A. Sørensen (1987), "Da chaperonen forsvandt", in *Den Jyske Historiker*, no. 41.
W. Owen (1913-18/1973), *War Poems and Others*, ed. by D. Hibberd, London.
A. Prost (1984), 'Les Monuments aux Morts. Culte républicain? Culte civique? Culte patriotique?', in P. Nora (ed.), *Les Lieux de Mémoire*. I: La Republique, Paris.
A. Prost (1986), 'Verdun', in P. Nora (ed.), *Les Lieux de Mémoire*. II: La Nation, Paris.
Punch (1919), *Mr. Punch's History of the Great War*, London.
D. Reynolds (1991), *Britannia Overruled*. British Policy & World Power in the 20th Century, London.
E. Raymond (1922), *Tell England*, London.
W.J. Reader (1988), *'At Duty's Call'*: A Study in Obsolete Patriotism, Manchester.
S. Sassoon (1928-37/1972), *The Complete Memoir of George Sherston*, London.
S. Sassoon (1915-34/1983), *The War Poems*, ed. by R. Hart-Davis, London.
N. A. Sørensen (1995), *Storbritanniens lange efterkrigstid 1918-1945*. Arbejdspapir fra Center for Kulturforskning, Aarhus Universitet.
A.J.P. Taylor (1965), *English History 1914-1945*, Penguin ed., Harmondsworth.
M. White (1998), "No Pardon for 'Deserters'", in *The Guardian*, July 25.
K. Wilson (1995), "Britain", in K. Wilson (ed.), *Decision for War, 1994*, London.
J.M. Winter (1995), *Sites of Memory, Sites of Mourning*. The First World War in European Cultural History, Cambridge.
R. Wohl (1979), *The Generation of 1914*, Cambridge, Mass.
A. Woollacott (1994), *On Her Their Lives Depend*. Munitions Workers in the Great War, Berkeley & L.A.
G. Wootton (1956), *The Official History of the British Legion*, London.

Imagining Scotland:
A Heritage Industry Examined*

David McCrone

Heritage is a thoroughly modern concept; it belongs to the final quarter of the twentieth century. It is true, of course, that heritage is as old as the world itself. Strictly speaking, heritage refers to that which has been or may be inherited, anything given or received to be a proper possession, an inherited lot or portion. But heritage has outgrown its legal definition. It has come to refer to a panoply of material and symbolic inheritances, some hardly older than the possessor. We have constructed heritage because we need to do so. Heritage is a condition of the late twentieth century.

When the British parliament passed the Ancient Monuments Act in 1882, it listed 68 monuments deemed to be significant. A century later, these numbered over 12,000. There were, in addition, 330,000 listed buildings, and in excess of 5000 conservation sites (Hewison, 1987). This growth in heritage, however, is largely a feature of the 1970s and 1980s. Half of Scotland's 400 museums have been opened since the late 1970s, and these attract around 12m visitors annually.

By the mid 1980s, tourism had become the UK's second biggest earner of foreign currency. By the late 1980s, 330 million site visits were being made, compared with 200 million in 1984. In Scotland, the key sites are Edinburgh Castle, and Glasgow's Art Gallery (with 1 million visitors each), the Burrell Collection (.75 million), around .5 million to the People's Palace in Glasgow, the same number to Edinburgh's Royal Museum of Scotland, and a third of a million to Holyroodhouse, to say nothing of the 350,000 which the Loch Ness Monster Exhibition claims to have had through its doors.

The explosion in heritage centres is a reflection of the demand for their products. Bodies such as The National Trust (covering England, Wales and Northern Ireland), the National Trust for Scotland, English Heritage, and Historic Scotland have large and important memberships. The National Trust enrolled its 2 millionth member in 1990 (its membership doubled in the 1980s) and is the largest conservation organisation in the world, which needs £80m per annum just to keep going at its present level, with a staff of over 2000, supplemented by 20,000 volunteers. By 1993, the Scottish organisation (NTS) had over 230,000 members, and an annual income of over £13m of which over £3m came from membership subscriptions.

Museums too have moved out of their musty past, and have been a major growth area in post-industrial Britain, with its attendant academic spin-off, 'the new museology' (the title of a collection of essays by Vergo in 1988). The Scottish Museums Council, for example, which is the main channel of central government support for the sector, supports over 300 local museums in Scotland, and has seen its annual allocation of grant aid rise from just £6000 in 1975/6 to almost £400,000 in the early 1990s.

Heritage and Authenticity

History like heritage has become less and less synonymous with professional historians and the realm of books. It is reflected in the shift from narrow scholarly appreciation towards history as a form of entertainment – or 'info-tainment' in the jargon. It also has employment pay-offs. To quote Robert Hewison, the heritage movement has been a godsend to the Manpower Services Commission, creating 'jobs that otherwise would not have existed, such as weaving, grinding corn, and living in a reproduction Iron Age round house at Manchester Museums' (1987: 102). Heritage presents new challenges as well as problems for academics such as historians and archaeologists. It is no longer enough to let the artefacts speak for themselves; indeed, it is vital that the artefacts speak. The demand is for authenticity rather than 'fact'. Peter Fowler points out that this frequently runs the risk of creating a past that never existed, and he quotes Joseph Heller's observation about a statue that 'it was an authentic Hellenistic imitation of a Hellenic reproduction ... for which there had never been an authentic original subject' (Fowler, 1992:13). But then again, he comments, 'there is more to the past than authenticity' (op.cit.:17).

The search for the authentic through heritage is aided by technological advances which allow more active participation for the spectator. People are now much more willing to 'dress up and do', by taking part in enactments of battles by joining the Sealed Knot Society, or role-playing in country house reconstructions. At its extreme, there is double reflexivity; tourists and natives perform their allocated roles for each other in the context of 'watching me watching you'. We may find that far-fetched and overly cynical until we remember the instance closer to home of the authenticity of tartan and the 'Scottish experience'. The desire to believe appears to overcome without much difficulty the counter-evidence that much of this 'tradition' is of recent origin. We can acknowledge pastiche while believing in it at the same time. Somehow, simulacra – what passes for the real – like the Scottish ceilidh experience have the power to overcome our cynicism.

Whether we are talking about actual or invented heritage sites, they have key features in common: they are, of course, places out of time for they operate in this time; they involve visits to 'time past'; they allow and encourage us to play for a time in another time; they seem to deny the possibility of decay and death for the passage of time is not allowed to occur between 'then' and 'now', and by implication 'we' and 'they' are not separated in time or, by definition, place. In this view, 'in these changing and disturbing times historic theme parks and heritage centres probably tell us as much about ourselves as about the past – indeed probably more' (Sorensen, 1989:65).

Understanding Scottish Heritage

Scotland mirrors the explosion in heritage which is taking place across the western world. There is another deeper and more important reason for studying heritage here. To put it simply, the whole idea of heritage has its origins in 19th century Scotland and the revolution in the writing of history brought about by Sir Walter Scott.

Scott's lifetime spanned a period of great historical change. In the words of Marinell Ash he lived through 'the tensions and contradictions of a traditional Scotland merging into a great world empire' (Ash, 1980:13). Scott spent part of his childhood on his grandfather's farm at Sandyknowe, near Smailholm in Roxburghshire and at an early age was exposed to the oral history tradition of the Borders. These early childhood experiences were to provide the inspiration for his novels. In these, Scott created a highly romantic and fictitious picture of the Scottish past. He then encouraged nineteenth century Scottish historians to recover and study historical documents and records and recreate for themselves similar pictures of the past. It was this activity which led the Hungarian philosopher Georg Lukacs to describe Scott's work as the first literary expression of world-historical consciousness.

Scott's historical revolution gave birth to a new way of thinking about the past which turned out to be extremely important in the context of nineteenth and early twentieth century European social development (Nairn, 1975). It introduced the idea of past and present as two very different entities. In the words of David Lowenthal: 'This new past gradually came to be cherished as a heritage that validated and exalted the present. And the new role heightened concern to save relics and restore monuments as emblems of communal identity, continuity and aspiration' (1985:xvi).

I will argue that there are special benefits to be had by looking at heritage from a Scottish perspective. Scotland is clearly a nation which is not a conventional state, and in which for much of its history of the last three hundred years its population has been very aware of the difference between its cultural and political identities. The view from the periphery is likely in this instance to be more insightful of processes taken for granted at the core.

It has been argued that Scotland suffers from too much heritage rather than too little. Its iconography includes tartan, Glencoe, Bonnie Prince Charlie and Culloden, Bannockburn, Burns, Mary Queen of Scots, whisky, Edinburgh Castle and much more. It is an *idée fixe* of many Scottish intellectuals that Scotland suffers from a deformation of its culture, that it has sold out its political birthright for a mess of cultural pottage (Nairn, 1975; Beveridge and Turnbull, 1989). They argue that instead of a rounded thought-world in which culture and politics work together in gear, the images of Scotland which have been let loose are adrift from their political moorings. All manner of imaginings have been allowed to gather around the representation of Scotland, of which perhaps the best-known is the Hollywood concoction, Brigadoon. Genuine Scottish culture has truly been 'eclipsed' (Beveridge and Turnbull, op. cit.).

At the centre of Scottish heritage stands the country itself, Scotland as theme-park. Its landscape is a social and cultural product. It is, in the words of Denis Cosgrove (1984) 'a way of seeing projected on to the land, and having its own techniques and compositional forms; a restrictive way of seeing that diminishes alternative modes of experiencing our relations with nature'.

The capture, both materially and culturally, of Highland estates in the 19th century for sporting purposes has bequeathed an iconography of Scottish landscape which is largely bereft of people. Landseer's best selling painting, the Monarch of the Glen, is a 'pastiche of the sublime' (Cosgrove, 1984:233) which nevertheless sets the framework for our expectations. Raymond Williams has pointed out that a working country is hardly ever a 'landscape' (Williams, 1973). Neither is it likely to be 'heritage'. The material power of the 19th century aristocracy and its monarchy was translated into the cultural representation of Scottish landscape. The 'stag at bay' image of the Highlands is probably so deeply embedded in our reading of the landscape that it makes radical land reform to restore it to a 'working' landscape all the more difficult. Cleared estates have come to represent landscape in Scotland, just as soldiers in kilts inform our image of what it is to be a Scot.

The power of heritage seems unduly onerous in Scotland. It seems at times as if Scotland only exists as heritage. What singles it out for distinction is the trappings of its past. Its modernity seems to make it little different from elsewhere. At a lecture in Aberdeen, I was once asked why I thought it had been so difficult to establish a heritage centre in the city devoted to North Sea oil. My answer was that this would not happen unless and until North sea oil was 'over' as an economic phenomenon. If Scotland is heritage-rich, then it could be because it has a past but not present or future. That is perhaps why many Scottish writers attack the cultural representations of Scotland as overly obsessed with what has passed, and why the nationalist party presents itself as a modernist, economistic one. Heritage in Scotland seems to many to be too tainted, too heavy.

It is, however, a crucial cultural repository for answers to the identity question. Like many 'stateless nations' such as Catalonia and Quebec, Scotland cannot rely on a pragmatic definition in terms of its political statehood. Indeed, given that it had no meaningful level of democratic control over its administration until 1999, it has even more of an identity crisis than the other two nations. There is no shortage of cultural accoutrements, however, in this search for collective identity. In spite of the high degree of institutional autonomy afforded to Scotland (Paterson, 1994), there is a continuous questing for identity. The old joke has it that Canadians are defined as a people who constantly pull up their roots to find out who they are. How much more does this apply to Scotland (and to Quebec and Catalonia) who do not have formal political sovereignty?

In the quest for national (as opposed to state) identity, heritage is a vital source of legitimacy. The iconography of nationalism is replete with sacred objects and places – flags, emblems, sites – often contested and fought over (like Jerusalem in Israel/Palestine, and Kosovo in Serbia/Albania). In asking who we are, the totems and icons of heritage are powerful signifiers of our identity. We may find tartanry, Bonnie Prince Charlie, Mary Queen of Scots, Bannockburn and Burns false descriptors of who we are, but they provide a source of ready-made distinguishing characteristics from England, our bigger, southern neighbour.

Heritage of this sort also communicates a powerful sense of glamour. We have grown accustomed to thinking of glamour as a fairly superficial show-biz quality of the late 20th century. It also has its deeper, more Scottish meaning of magic or delusion. The glamour of an object originally referred in the 18th century to its magical powers, to enchantment and witchcraft, even the power to bamboozle or deceive. Its etymology derives from the same root as 'grammar' – 'grimoire' – a sorcerer's book (Oxford English Dictionary). The painter Allan Ramsay is quoted in OED as defining glamour as follows: 'when devils, wizards or jugglers deceive the sight, they are said to cast glamour o'er the eyes of the spectator', and Sir Walter Scott, who did so much to create Scottish heritage, is attributed with using it to refer to delusive or alluring charm.

Understanding Scottish Heritage: the Iconography of Place

When it comes to tourism, the Scottish tourist industry presents Scotland as a 'land out of time', as an 'enchanted fortress in a disenchanted world' (Rojek, 1993:181). This, of course, is a ploy common to all tourist bodies in all countries. What is the point of selling the same as back home? A 'foreign' country is meant to be the opposite of the immediate conditions of 'home'; the exact contrary of disorder, tumult, the unexpected.

Scotland has one major feature which allows this presentation, its association with the 'wilderness'. And wilderness is presented as the antithesis of culture, as the quintessential escape area in modern society. After all, the claim is that Scotland is the last great European wilderness. The key to the 'wilderness' tag is that it is a social construction. By the end of the 18th century the Highlands were discovered as a scenic game park replete with 'nature, – and its game – salmon, deer and grouse. Such has been the re-construction of the Highlands in particular that we find it impossible to 'see' them in any other way. They have, in Womack's words, been 'colonised by an empire of signs' (1989:1). He points out that whereas 'botanically no doubt 'calluna vulgaris' [heather] is exactly as it was in the 1730s, semiotically it has been irrevocably hybridised' (ibid.: 2), namely that it has been given a social meaning evoking Highland and, through it, Scottish culture.

From even a cursory reading of Scottish and Highland history it is clear that the cultural construction of the region was the result of political and commercial forces, often acting together. What undoubtedly had been a distinctive region in geographical, linguistic and economic terms before and after the Union of 1707 was invested with cultural qualities and meanings. These meanings were not generated randomly but were the result of double defeats – first from a lowland-dominated Scottish state, and after 1745 and the Culloden defeat, by a wider British political system. The distinction between the Lowlands and the Highlands has always been a shifting and contentious one in practice, given that the linguistic, economic and geographical boundaries do not coincide with each other. There is, however, little doubting the cultural divide in the sense that the Highlands were invested with symbolism of being 'foreign' and exotic. The irony is that by the end of the 18th century Scotland as a whole was being colonised by this powerful sign.

By the end of the 18th century, then, the elements were in place for the construction of modern tourist icons. From then on, and especially in their literary exploitation by Walter Scott in the early decades of the 19th century, the Highlands in particular became the focus for 're-discovery' of the wilderness. Mairi MacArthur observes that visitors in 1883 remarked that 'the farther we went the more we were reminded that to travel in Scotland is to travel through the Waverley novels' (1993:23). Guidebooks and travel memoirs highlighted three themes: the wild grandeur of the landscape, remoteness and peace, with a dash of romantic (preferably tragic) history.

We are dealing here with what the geographer Denis Cosgrove has called 'terrains of power' (1994). He observes: 'Nature, landscape and environment are semiotic signifiers, deeply embedded in the cultural constitution of individual European nations and integral to the distinctive identities of Europe's peoples'. The point he is making is that these 'constitutions' relate to systems of power, not in any predetermined way, but as ideological constructs which reflect, often in attenuated ways, its operation. The 'imagined geography' of England focuses on 'woods of downland pastures of SE England's 'home counties', 'Constable' country in Suffolk and Wiltshire water meadows, and the hawthorn-squared ploughlands of the Midland counties'. On the other hand, 'Welsh and Scottish nationalisms have constructed their own meaning from mountain landscapes, valleys and glens, drawing as heavily on the natural world as upon their separate language to construct differences from England'.

This is an important point. It is not simply that the iconography of the Highlands or of Scotland carries a unique message which speaks only to the powerful who might use it as a holiday playground. The iconography 'leaks' in such a way that it can be turned to radical uses, in respective nationalist and oppositional discourses. 'The wee bit hill and glen' of the anthem 'Flower of Scotland' may make weak poetry but strong politics. The ability of different political forces to 'read' into the landscape a suitable message is the key here. It is not that only one message can be read off the heritage signs, or that the viewer can read in what he or she wants. The signification is not 'depthless'. Rather, the imaginative bonds between 'nature' and 'nation' are deep across Europe.

The nub of my argument is that heritage is significant in Scotland because it rests on a national, cultural, dimension. Heritage is a reflection of nationalism in its widest sense. It may not, and frequently does not, carry political overtones, as the observations of life-members of the National Trust for Scotland makes clear. You do not have to be a Scottish Nationalist to be a cultural nationalist, although as we will argue later in this chapter, it has become increasingly more difficult to separate the cultural and political realms in modern Scotland. The conclusion of some writers that 'her [Scotland's] political identity lost, her cultural identity began to be absorbed' (Pittock, 1991:72) does not strike us as a proper reading of the evidence.

Manufacturing Scottish Heritage

There are three major competing discourses on Scottish heritage. First, it is treated as a product to be sold in the marketplace. This manipulation of heritage evokes the vocabulary of commerce, and is largely the preserve of the Scottish Tourist Board (STB). We will examine the assumptions about and presentations of Scottish heritage by STB. The second discourse concerning heritage is that of inheritance, or *'patrimoine'*. This evokes a vocabulary of social and cultural order, and is most closely associated with the National Trust for Scotland, with its strongly patrician ethos and culture. In the broadest sense, this is a 'political' discourse on heritage. The third discourse is more strongly associated with the 'academy', with the vocabulary of technique and knowledge, and we will examine the role of Historic Scotland and its concern with artefacts and ruins as a fitting representative of this discourse.

These three bodies constitute the 'holy trinity' of Scottish heritage: the Scottish Tourist Board, Historic Scotland, and the National Trust for Scotland. They work alongside each other, but have distinct aims and purposes, and quite different organisational cultures. They are set within a political and cultural framework which includes government departments and private operators. At the state level, The Scottish Office provides most of the funding for heritage which it dispenses indirectly through its public agencies such as the Scottish Tourist Board (STB), which receives three-quarters of its budget from the Scottish Office, Historic Scotland (80%), Scottish Museums Council (72%), and Scottish Natural Heritage (100%). Only the National Trust for Scotland (NTS) does not receive funds directly from the state, although it is a major recipient of grant in aid from Historic Scotland for the upkeep of many of its properties. Further down the heritage chain, private and commercial operators of 'stately homes', independent as well as local authority museums, receive grants from state agencies like Historic Scotland and the Scottish Museums Council. The heritage industry in Scotland has a strong 'voluntary sector' ethos (in contrast, for example, to that in France with its historic sense of national *patrimoine*), but it is clear that it would not survive without public funds.

Tourism and Heritage

We can gauge Scottish Tourist Board's approach to heritage from two sources: the images it presents; and what it says about Scotland's heritage. STB advertising campaigns stress landscapes and locations. Its television projects recently include the 'talking eagles' whereby two eagles fly down a Scottish loch discussing why there is no better place to be; and 'Mull early closing' in which a shopkeeper closes early in order to go fishing with friends – this also has a Gaelic version, and both are on offer in mainland Scotland. STB has also exploited the posters industry under its campaign, 'One Visit is Never Enough'. The poster industry is a lucrative and important part of late twentieth century tourism indicating (or implying) the message of 'been there, done that', and posters become the accoutrements of travel like T-shirts and key rings.

STB posters attempt to convey particular images of Scotland

- Peopleless places- the landscape: This is the stuff of Romantic representations with 'nature' presented as wild, rugged, barren, beau-

tiful. The dominant colours are blues, browns, white. The lochs are deep, calm, and always brooding.
- Majestic Scotland: castles, kilts, pipers. Edinburgh Castle is the icon associated most strongly by tourists and by natives with Scotland.
- 'Everyday' Scotland: the posters of post boxes and of curlers convey the everyday melding into the exotic. Strange games played on ice by men in kilts; post boxes miniaturised in strange locations. Low and high heritage blur in the manner described by the French minister for culture: '... it is no longer cold stones or of exhibits kept under glass in museum cabinets. It now includes the village washhouses, the little country church, local songs and forms of speech, crafts and skills' (Hoyau, 1988:28).

The other insight into the STB conception of heritage comes from a major report it commissioned in 1989 from an associate member of the international consultants Arthur Young International. This report formed the basis of an STB publication 'Visitor Attractions: a development guide', aimed at entrepreneurs interested in setting up or developing visitor attractions, including heritage sites. The remit of the heritage study is worth reproducing in full because it indicates STB's definition of heritage. Heritage attractions, it spells out:

are intrinsically related to the Scottish
- landscape
- history or
- way of life

can be presented in a way which will

- attract and satisfy visitors
- generate income and employment and
- help to conserve the features to which the attractions relate.

The key elements of this definition are that heritage attractions:

- must have core elements which are intrinsic to Scotland in some significant way

- *need to be concerned solely with history and the past* (our emphasis)

- must be linked directly to visitor use and economic benefit and to conservation.
(STB 'Visitor Attractions: a development guide', no date, 47 pp.)

This account is interesting for a number of reasons. First, it gives priority to commercial aspects ('generate income and employment', versus *'help to* conserve the features...'). Second, and more significantly, there is a curious contradiction between the terms of reference for the Heritage Attractions Study commissioned by the STB International and Planning Division, and the subsequent publication whose definition of heritage is spelled out above. Whereas one of the key elements in the above is that heritage attractions 'need to be concerned solely with history and the past' (see italicised above), the terms of reference for the study itself says precisely the opposite: 'need *not* be concerned solely with history and the past'. We have been unable to find out how this *volte face* arose, but from the tenor of the consultants' report, it is plain that 'history and the past' are not deemed necessary in developing heritage attractions. We can only surmise that in the final publication, its producer assumed that history and heritage were the same thing, whereas the gist of the consultants' report was that the economic potential lay precisely in the *lack* of correspondence between heritage and history.

Are we to assume that these are simply 'creative ideas' to stimulate the consultants' sponsors about heritage? The fact that STB included it in the remit perhaps implies that these ideas are the wider reaches of the heritage industry, but not by much. The using of 'living history' techniques, with the stress on 'the magic of the real', authenticity rather than history, historic enactments, actor role-playing, outdoor theatre are to be found in many other heritage projects and in other societies. Thinking the unthinkable out loud is frequently a device for testing the waters in the marketplace, especially if we remember that the development guide produced by STB is aimed at developers and operators of what it calls 'heritage attractions'. We might think that we are looking at the Scottish heritage experience of the millennium. However, in 1994, a proposal was announced to open a £3m Neolithic heritage park near Oyne, a village of 200 people, in Aberdeenshire. The main attraction was to be a 900 square metre grass covered dome, approached by a time tunnel to put visitors in the pre-history mood using interactive displays, laser shows and video walls. The park itself was to include mock iron Age houses, a neolithic long house, and a Roman camp. The whole project was funded by the local council and Scottish Enterprise. About the same time Historic Scotland announced that its pre-historic hill-fort and burial mound at Cairnpapple near Bathgate would not be open in the coming season as the number of visitors was unlikely to warrant it. Fiction, it seems, is more palatable, or profitable, than truth.

Managing the State's Heritage: Historic Scotland

'Scotland has a rich legacy from the past – a heritage of monuments and buildings which bear silent witness to our proud history stretching back over 5000 years, which are a delight to us today and which we must carefully preserve for future generations.'

In using these words in its first framework document, the-then Conservative Secretary of State for Scotland, Ian Lang, was setting the agenda for this executive agency to manage the nation's built heritage. If the Scottish Tourist Board treats heritage as a product, and uses the vocabulary of commerce, then Historic Scotland defines heritage much more as artefact, and speaks the vocabulary of technique. Historic Scotland, however, has, like British Rail, succumbed to business-speak by referring to its users as 'customers'

Although it was not christened Historic Scotland until 1991, this body, along with English heritage and CADW Wales came into being in 1984. All three bodies were products of the National Heritage Act 1983 which was fuelled by Mrs Thatcher's desire to make the organisations responsible for protecting traditional heritage more commercially minded.

Historic Scotland avoided sounding like a belated carbon-copy of English Heritage, something which the organisation actively wished to avoid. Similarly in keeping with the new times, the defensively sounding 'warders' of properties became user-friendly 'custodians', swapping prison officers' garb for more informal tartan trews and jumpers.

Historic Scotland has a budget of some £30 million (80% from the state, and the rest self-generated) which has virtually doubled since 1984, with running costs for 1993-4 at £12.7 million. These figures put it on a par with the Scottish Tourist Board. Visitors to its seventy sites have risen in that period from 1.8 million per annum to 2.4 million, and its membership organisation, Friends of Historic Scotland, stands at around 30,000.

The popularising of Scottish heritage has focused on literature and advertising, both press and television. The 'Scotland' which is presented in the literature is clear-cut and action-based. What kind of Scotland is it? It is described thus:

> Scotland is a land of castles. Mighty fortresses on rocky heights, isolated keeps, elegant homes for great families and grim strongholds set on towering sea cliffs.
>
> These were the stages on which the dynasties of Bruce, Douglas and Stewart played out their power struggles; where William Wallace fought for Scotland's independence, and Mary Queen of Scots fought for her life.
>
> In the great halls, great men discussed affairs of state against backdrops of regal splendour. Behind the scenes, whispered plots and counterplots were hatched, while in the gloom of the dungeons, unfortunate wretches ended their lives in misery and despair.
>
> Noble men and tyrants, kings and queens, lords and commoners all made their entrances and exits, and now only the stones remain to speak centuries of drama. (Historic Scotland 'The Popular Choice')

This pamphlet with its revealing title 'The Popular Choice' is a long way from the technicalities of medieval ruins. The text continues with descriptions such as: 'ruthless political intrigue', 'buccaneering raids', 'wayward churchman', 'burning and looting', 'a rare sense of tranquility'. Its history is fairly nationalist and masculinist: the Jacobite Risings are not 'rebellions'; there is 'the ruthlessness of the Hanoverian forces', the Highlanders were 'too loyal to take the gold offered for Bonnie Prince Charlie'; there is whisky-smuggling, harsh punishment for soldiers, and all in all, 'real stories for real men' (sic). The implicit message seems aimed at fathers taking young sons on boisterous days-out at castles. This is backed-up by the agency's own focus-group research: it shows that 'the 'stories' of the history of Scotland are of great interest to the audience. The message should use 'colour', fun, and excitement rather than text-book style teaching.' The research showed that there was less difference between AB social categories (managerial and administrative workers) and C2s (skilled manual workers).

The research led to a series of television and newspaper adverts. These ads were designed to be witty and eyecatching. The TV campaign which ran in the summer of 1991 showed two gargoyles engaged in witty repartee. Historic Scotland's budget did not stretch to a 1992 campaign. The newspaper adverts used cartoon drawing and witty commentary such as 'King comfortably enthroned at Linlithgow Palace', 'What kind of person carves his name on the wall of a 16th century abbey?' [answer: the architect]; and 'Waverley man finds Crown jewels in spare room' [Walter Scott's discovery of Scotland's Crown Jewels at Edinburgh Castle in 1818].

Historic Scotland is protected by a broad nationalist discourse in Scotland. It would be hard to envisage a similar controversy to the one which engulfed English Heritage in 1992 when it proposed to sell off its less profitable assets. This is not because Historic Scotland does not have any of these, because only Edinburgh Castle, and to a far lesser extent Stirling Castle, are profitable in their own right. Given the weakness of the Tory Party in Scotland, the Scottish Office would also have found it very difficult to appoint a Conservative businessman to lead Historic Scotland in the way that it did south of the border.

Nation in Trust: the National Trust for Scotland

If the Scottish Tourist Board represents heritage as product, and Historic Scotland heritage as artefact, then the National Trust for Scotland (NTS) interprets heritage as inheritance. Its vocabulary is that of organic order, and contrasts with STB's language of commerce, and Historic Scotland's vocabulary of technique. For example, the chairman of the NTS council commented in his forward to the 1993 annual report: '... our heritage – whether it be the built heritage or the heritage of countryside and wilderness – is part of the soul of the nation and we ignore the nation's soul at our peril.'

It is hard to imagine either STB or Historic Scotland making a play to be keepers of the national soul. What makes this doubly odd is that NTS is not an agency of government but a charitable 'trust' (in setting up the National Trust in England in 1895, Octavia Hill preferred the word 'trust' to 'company' in order to stress the benevolent aspect of the operation). It is this ethos of voluntarism which helps to give heritage in Britain its image of good works and service, although in terms of funding it is likely that the state is by far the major contributor.

From the outset, NTS has had a strong aristocratic and landed domination of its council. Its first president was the Duke of Atholl (1932-1942), who was succeeded by Sir John Stirling Maxwell (1944-1954), who had served as a vice-president from 1932 until 1943, and who was also chairman of the Royal Commission on the Ancient and Historical Monuments of Scotland (RCAHM) from 1940 until 1949. There was no president of the council after Maxwell until The Earl of Wemyss and March succeeded in 1968 and served until 1991, when he gave way to the Marquess of Bute (Wemyss succeeded Maxwell as chairman of RCAHM in 1949 until 1985 when he in turn was succeeded by the Earl of Balcarres). Neither can we interpret the presidency as mere figure-head. Chairmen of the Council have all been male, and titled persons served for the first fifty years of the Trust's history: Sir Iain Colquhoun (from 1932-1945), The Earl of Wemyss and March (1946-1968), and the Marquess of Bute (1969-1984). He was succeeded by WM Cuthbert (1985-1989), and by RC Tyrell (from 1990 until 1994). The chairman-designate of NTS, Hamish Leslie Melville, is an Eton and Oxford-educated financier who owns an estate in Garve, Ross-shire.

Vice-presidents have also been drawn heavily from lairds and gentry. Only in more recent years have non-titled persons begun to appear on the council. The remarkable feature of this list is the overwhelming preponderance of the titled, the landed and the powerful. Only three women have been vice-presidents, and only from the late 1970s.

In a country like Scotland where the land question has been an integral part of its political agenda, it might seem to be a disadvantage for the Trust to be so dominated by lairds and gentry. The Trust has worked to offset this by stressing its ideology of stewardship and social responsibility. The Trust presents an ethos of organic conservatism, and of a society in which the laird's house and the little houses are integrated in an organic whole so that all have their part to play in the scheme of things. This does not mean, of course, that all mix freely.

What sort of image of Scottish heritage does the trust convey? In keeping with its patrician image, it is a traditional, 'respectable' one, eschewing any downmarket iconography of Scotland, as befits a gentry-led organisation. Its magazine, 'Heritage Scotland', is douce and worthy. An editorial by the director in the 1993 Summer edition begins:

> We regularly read newspaper headlines denouncing the 'moral sickness' within our society. It is therefore important to all of us to know that somebody cares. It is also important to know that there are caring organisations like the National Trust for Scotland, which not only preserves and protects buildings and inanimate objects, but also cares for the people and the communities at its properties. *The trust is very conscious of its responsibilities in its role in the community. The Trust is, itself, a community but it is also part of a wider community which it seeks to serve through its duty to act 'for the benefit of the nation* (our emphasis). (Heritage Scotland, Summer 1993, 10,2:10).

I have focused on the key agencies involved in Scottish heritage. Each has their own carefully constructed rhetoric and vocabulary. Whereas the Scottish Tourist Board are closest to a market conception of heritage and the vocabulary of commerce ('Scotland's For Me!'), Historic Scotland forefronts the heritage of artefacts ('Don't believe it when they tell you stones can't speak'), while concentrating on technical expertise. As we have seen, the National Trust for Scotland employs the language of conservative nationalism ('our heritage is part of the soul of the nation').

An examination of heritage sites in Scotland reveals an apparent conundrum. Why, in the Scottish Borders, one of the most fertile part of Scotland, does the National Trust for Scotland have so few properties? The answer to our puzzle is not that the borderlands are bereft of heritage, but that the key ones are in private hands. They are the great stately homes of the 'mighty magnates' of Scotland. Here is the private face of heritage.

Heritage and the Landed Elite

The conventional way of explaining the capture of heritage for commercial purposes by the owners of the stately homes industry is that this has become an economic necessity in a modern world which is not of their financial and ideological making. There is truth in this, but I will argue that there is more to it than that.

If we consider landowners in general as a status group rather than as a class per se, then we can begin to chart their continuous struggle to hold the line of social privilege. Without denying that they have used their property assets as productive resources, it seems that their social behaviour can be better understood within the framework I have outlined. For example, concern with lifestyle of the 'gentleman', with the proper ways of behaving, with 'noblesse oblige', and correctness of rituals and beliefs does reveal the principles of status honour rather than class advantage.

The conventional wisdom about the 'stately home' industry is that it is largely a financial device to maintain the great houses by state and voluntary means. There is clearly truth in this, but not the whole of it. The inclusion of the word 'home' helps to evoke the private as well as the public domains, just as 'house' describes the family and its name as well as its relationship to its property – titles, residences, heirlooms and land. The word 'seat', for example, clearly implies residence. But many lairds have their homes elsewhere, often in London. Nevertheless, as Wright points out, the symbolism of 'home' has been used to romanticise the patriarchal family, to idolise domestic drudgery, and to vaunt a national heritage of 'stately homes' (1985:11).

The stately home heritage industry allows the lairds to insinuate their own history into that of the Scottish and British nations. While having distinct identities as Scottish lairds – 'authenticated' by family names, crests, mottos, tartans and clans – they have much in common with great landowners south of the border. It is not uncommon to find a Scottish laird owning land in England, and vice versa.

Stately home guidebooks provide the ideal format for this interweaving, with their manicured family trees, tracing family antecedents back in genealogical time to the great figures of Scottish and English history. If the nation's history can be told through the medium of the family biography, then one cannot destroy the one without the other. The family and the country become one.

The Duke of Buccleuch 'owns' the lands around Ettrick Forest because they were bestowed upon his ancestors in return for services to Robert the Bruce [Scottish credentials] in the fourteenth century. At the same time, the Duke is, in the words of the Buccleuch guidebook, only 'a life trustee dedicated to the constant improvement of a vital asset to the benefit of everyone concerned, as well as further generations of his own family, on whom the responsibility for future progress rests.' The guidebook, then, is not simply a guide to the layout of the family property, but a chronological narrative of how the dynasty came to occupy the positions it holds. The guidebook continues:

> Once the links in the chain of continuity are broken, through the irreversible process of the break-up of estates, the merits of multiple land-use are lost forever. The advantage of continuity spanning many generations apply just as much to the families of those who occupy let farms and estate employees. On Buccleuch estates some family partnerships between landlord and tenant go back possibly as far as the 12th century.

Thus, the ideology of land and landownership is intricately connected and interwoven with a theory of history in a vernacular and informal sense, and with a theory of everyday life. The Buccleuchs are able to exploit the ambiguity of the term 'nation'. While their works of art are part of the British 'national' heritage, their connections with Bruce and with Douglas (the family name associated with Drumlanrig in the western borders) make their Scottish credentials abundantly clear. The Buccleuchs and their fellow lairds see themselves as champions of 'history' rather than as captains of a heritage industry. In this regard, Sir Walter Scott played a crucial role not simply in 'heritagising' Scotland, but in weaving into the 'story' of Scotland the Buccleuchs whom he vested with the (inauthentic) honour of being his own 'clan chief'. Whereas those who had access to the trappings of a Highland culture could play the clan chief, Scott was investing his own lowland namesake with the title too. To do so may have made poor history, but good politics.

In a country where the lairds and the land question have a salience in politics of some significance, and in the context of Scotland's place in the British state being questioned as never before, Scotland's lairds appear to have succeeded in converting their own and the nation's history into commodities whereby they can save themselves.

Conclusion: Ethnicity, Identity and Heritage

Heritage has uncommon power in Scotland because it is a stateless nation. It is not the case that only formal political power, ultimately sovereignty, is the only guarantee of nationhood. The political slogan 'A nation once again' is inaccurate because since the Union of 1707 Scotland has not ceased to be a nation. In large part its institutional autonomy as a distinctive civil society, with its holy trinity of law, education and religion, has helped to underwrite the continuing and strong sense of national identity north of the border (Paterson, 1994).

In Scotland the weight of identity has been placed conventionally since the Union on cultural rather than political matters. We might reflect, for example, on the claim of the former Conservative politician, Ian Lang, that Bannockburn was the key event in Scottish history. It may seem somewhat strange to find the representative of a Unionist party claiming this sacred nationalist icon. The key lies in his final comments:

> From then on [after Bannockburn] as a nation, we have never looked back. So much so that it was our king James IV (sic) who succeeded to the throne of England in 1603: and it was his great grand-daughter – another Scot – who oversaw the Union of the nations of Scotland and England in 1707. This is the real legacy of Bannockburn, and it is one of which I am very proud. That is why I would like to have been there in 1314. (The Scotsman, 27 November 1993)

This claim that Unionism and Nationalism are reconciled in this way may strike our eyes in the late 20th century as somewhat odd. We have grown accustomed to an antithesis between them, at least as they are expressed in conventional political forms, between the Conservative party and the Scottish National Party. The dominant wisdom in contemporary Scotland is that Scottishness and Conservatism are strange bed-fellows.

In the mid-19th century a view prevailed that only because Scotland won and retained her Independence in 1314 was she able to enter the Union of 1707 as an equal partner, with England, in the British state. The National Association for the Vindication of Scottish Rights, for example, which was founded in 1853 expressed a sense of patriotism which allowed it to proclaim admiration for its partner England. Similarly, the erection of the monument in Edinburgh to Walter Scott which was begun in 1833 stresses the Scottish contribution to English heritage. And perhaps more surprisingly (given Scott's political Toryism) those who raised funds for the erection of monuments to the two prime Scottish patriots William Wallace and Robert the Bruce did so by stressing the contribution to the Union (Morton, 1993).

Such a discourse seems to contemporary Scottish ears anachronistic, because political developments in the 20th century make the separation of 'nation' from 'state' less and less possible. We have grown used to the state encroaching on civil society, and civil society making increasing demands on the state. The cultural and political dimensions become increasingly fused. We have seen that there is a considerable body of opinion which celebrates Scottish heritage while giving allegiance to Conservatism. We have seen too that heritage is not some distant cultural hobby, but has the power to define who one is in a historical sense. Heritage in Scotland has the power not only to mobilise politically but to define who people are to themselves and others. In this respect Scotland's past has a vibrant if indeterminate future.

---

* This chapter is drawn from *Scotland – the Brand: the Making of Scottish Heritage,* published by Edinburgh University Press, 1995.

Bibliography

Ash, M. (1980) *The Strange Death of Scottish History*, Edinburgh.
Beveridge, C. & Turnbull, R. (1989) *The Eclipse of Scottish Culture*, Edinburgh.
Cosgrove, D. (1984) *Social Formation and Symbolic Landscape*, London.
Cosgrove, D. (1994) 'Terrains of Power', in *Times Higher Education Supplement*, 11 March.
Fowler, P. J. (1992) *The Past in Contemporary Society: then, now*, London.
Hewison, R. (1987) *The Heritage Industry: Britain in a Climate of Decline*, London.
Hoyau, P. (1988) 'Heritage and "the conserver society" French case', in Lumley, R., (ed.) *The Museum Time Machine*, London.
Lowenthal, D. (1985) *The Past is a Foreign Country*, Cambridge.
MacArthur, M. (1993) 'Blasted Heaths and Hills of Mist', in *Scottish Affairs*, 3.
McCrone, D., Morris, A. and Kiely, R. (1995) *Scotland – the Brand: the Making of Scottish heritage*, Edinburgh.
Morton, G. (1993) *Unionist-Nationalism: The Historical Construction of Scottish National Identity, Edinburgh 1830-1860*, PhD Thesis: University of Edinburgh.
Nairn, T. (1975) 'Old Nationalism and New Nationalism' in Brown, G., (ed.), (1975), *The Red Paper on Scotland*, Edinburgh.
Paterson, L. (1994) *The Autonomy of Modern Scotland*, Edinburgh.
Pittock, M. (1991) *The Invention of Scotland: the Stuart Myth and the Scottish Identity, 1638 to the present*, London.
Rojek, C. (1993) *Ways of Escape*, London.
Sorensen, C. (1988) 'Theme Parks & Time Machines' in Vergo, P. (ed.), *The New Museology*, London.
Williams, R. (1973) *The Country and the City*, London.
Womack, P. (1989) *Improvement and Romance: Constructing the Myth of the Highlands*, London.
Wright, P. (1985) *On Living in an Old Country: The National Past in Contemporary Britain*, London.
Vergo, P. (ed.) (1988) *The New Museology*, London.

Facts and Greasy Piglets: An Essay on Historiography and Fiction

Lars Ole Sauerberg

>…some pranksters at an end-of-term dance released into the hall a piglet which had been smeared with grease. It squirmed between legs, evaded capture, squealed a lot. People fell over trying to grasp it, and were made to look ridiculous in the process. The past often seems to behave like that piglet.[1]

The quotation is from Julian Barnes's *Flaubert's Parrot*, his playful and intertext-saturated novel from 1984 devoted to the investigation of the nature of reality, memory and the past. Trying to find the parrot which inspired Flaubert to write the short story 'Un coeur simple,' the retired Dr Braithwaite has eventually to realize that any one of a large number of stuffed parrots from the local Museum of Natural History may have been the one borrowed by Flaubert for his creative needs.

The nature of the past is just as elusive as Flaubert's parrot. When we trace events of the past, we try to find the hard evidence left to us – in the form of texts, pictures, monuments and artefacts – and to interpret and combine it in ways that we consider sensible, whether we belong to the school of accurate restoration of the past or to the school of assessing the significance of the past for the present.

The monopoly and privilege of the historian to dig into and interpret the past on the basis of empirical data has been increasingly questioned in recent years. Those who deal with the philosophy of historiography and with the theory of literary texts often express the view that it is problematic to maintain a view of structural or mimetic difference between texts produced by those who tell a *history* and those who tell a *story*.

Historians have a hard time trying to catch the essence of what they are dealing with. Napoleon comes over to us in so many shapes, but never the fully facetted one which was the man himself. Compare again Julian Barnes on the subject of biography:

> The trawling net fills, then the biographer hauls it in, sorts, throws back, stores, fillets and sells. Yet consider what he doesn't catch: there is always far more of that. The biography stands, fat and worthy-burgherish on the shelf, boastful and sedate: a shilling life will give you all the facts, a ten pound one all the hypotheses as well. But think of everything that got away, that fled with the last deathbed exhalation of the biographee. What chance would the craftiest biographer stand against the subject who saw him coming and decided to amuse himself?[2]

In fiction writers attempt to provide and retain that personal essence which fled with the last deathbed exhalation. They have recreated historical figures, even to the point where the fictive creation has completely replaced the historical. Just consider the case of Richard III, whose claim to everlasting life depends significantly on the dramatic business of a certain English Renaissance dramatist.

And writers of fiction create a multitude of beings who might have existed in the world as we know it, but who didn't, although we feel strongly that they are part of our past as we are aware of it in the now. Characters like Oliver Twist or Mrs Dalloway come to mind immediately. Each of them figures whom many of us consider of the very essence of their times.

The traditional distinction between the fictional and the nonfictional is, as the terms imply, a matter of assuming a categorical distinction between factuality and fictionality. A fictional narrative is non-factual in the sense that it does not necessarily correspond to actual events or persons. In contrast the nonfictional text reflects a state of affairs existing independently of the existence of any text. However, the precariousness of this distinction has been a matter for insistent comment since the structuralists pointed to the general structuration of meaning. Deconstructionists, in their radical application of structuralist insight, as well as critical metahistorians, have stressed the dependence of signification on textuality and writing. Historians working along strictly empirical lines will claim that the truth of their work consists in the possibility of checking it against the sources employed. But these sources themselves are documents, that is texts already results of a prior process of interpretation or rendering into signification. In his effort to get to the bottom of a problem the historian, by critical comparison of documents relating to the same matter, will arrive at the 'objective historical fact,' a phenomenon whose ontological nature is more complex than most empirical historians will allow.

Belief in an objectively founded difference between fact and fiction and in our ability to distinguish unproblematically between them is a commonly accepted premise of our sense of history. It is as if we think that our historical awareness results directly from the contemplation of historical data either by direct confrontation with 'facts' or as mediated in histories. The facts or data are felt to be stored without interference in a kind of master file in some rational part of the mind. Once there, of course, the historical data may in Coleridgean fashion become the raw material for the imagination to work on, but the objectivity and the rationality of our approach to the data remain untainted. Although this positivist view must be assumed to be still widely accepted by today's reading public, it is hardly tenable once we begin to scrutinize the phenomenology of history.

Historical facts are available as non-textual forms (excavations, monuments, kitchen and handicraft utensils, etc.) and textual (peace treaties, correspondence, chronicles, etc.). The professional historian will use both kinds of source material, and as the result of this use of them he will fabricate a (new) text. However neutral the historian considers himself in his transformation of research data into the learned article, his very use of language and the very act of writing, understood as the continuous process of formulating and editing, will already have corrupted the assumed neutrality. But the neutrality of the facts has actually been challenged long before the historian gets to work in his study. If he is dealing with textual material, a writing process will already have been at work interpreting the facts. The lapidary chronicles of medieval scribes are an illustrative case of extreme selectivity perforce guiding the historian in his assessment of what is important and what is not important.[3] Non-textual historical facts might be expected to be above such a priori interpretation, but even the archaeologist discovering an ancient body long immersed in a peat-bog is bound to get inextricably mixed up in a kind of bog-corpse 'intertextuality:' the body will seem to signal its parallels to earlier finds, but the parallels are part of archaeological hypotheses, formed by the evidence of the bodies found.

Most people do not want or need to define their historical awareness exclusively on the basis of immediate source knowledge, but will point to the historical textbook – or the learned essay or monograph if particularly interested in a certain subject – as the source of their historical awareness. In the case of the non-specialised but interested lay reader, his historical awareness typically results from a text which is the last in a line of increasingly generalized and comprehensive re-writings of other texts, say the history section in a tourist guide or a TV feature, in combination with impressions from sight-seeing, visits to museums, etc. For most people the sense of history is the result a highly compounded input of perceptions and impressions, to which art should be added, since art plays a significant if often neglected role for the formation of the historical awareness.

Even if the sources on which Shakespeare based his plays are still available, and conveniently so in scholarly editions of the plays, it is Shakespeare's imaginative renderings of figures and events which have taken root in the public mind. The process does not end with Shakespeare, however, but with famous actors' interpretations of parts. Lord Olivier's Richard III, for example, has no doubt become the 'real' king despite attempts by learned historians to offer more facetted and differently emphasized portraits. The same is true of figures such as the Roman emperor Claudius, who lives on in Robert Graves's interpretation, and, at a further remove, in the English actor Derek Jacoby's interpretation of Graves's interpretation in the TV serial. Examples of this double (or triple, really, since the historical document must also be considered an interpretation) rendering are legion. And there is the host of artistic representations of the past, with the medieval habit of representing classical Biblical figures in contemporary clothing as an example of interpretation carried to (admittedly unintentional) extremes. For how many of us is Michelangelo's Moses not the Moses of the Old Testament, and the scenarios of Cecil B. de Mille not the proper settings of ancient Israel and Rome? With the mass-media predilection for drama documentaries the supply of such highly individual representations of past factuality – or rather corporate, given the collective nature of the modern entertainment industry – is quickly growing.[4]

In the perspective of the discourse seen as a verbal construct there seems to be very little, if indeed any, difference between the historical account and the work of fiction. As presentations of and comment on some kind of action, both kinds of discourse employ action, character, and perspective. It is true that in fiction all events and characters are usually imaginary. But even in the most wildly fabulating or the most devastatingly deconstructive metafictional text there is some resemblance to the assumption of experienced reality, at least as something to react against. And the dividing line between the real and the imagined becomes increasingly blurred with time. Only a contemporary audience will be in a position to appreciate the distinction, as in the case when a *roman à clef* is felt to have an offensive effect by introducing the reader to imaginative misrepresentations of something generally accepted as factual knowledge. As time passes and the possibilities for immediate verification diminish, the area of factual knowledge is reduced to the historical events recorded in the standard histories from which most of us learn our history, that is in most cases primary- and secondary-school textbooks. By and large this means an outline of the past in terms of the highlights in military, diplomatic, ecclesiastical and royal history. If the novelist steps into history, say in the fifteen-thirties presenting his hero as a loyal monk trying to save precious relics from the confiscations of Henry VIII, there is an enormous grey area open to imaginative padding. The technique of the historical novelist is precisely to fill the gaps in received knowledge with events and characters absent from but not incompatible with the known records. From the point of view of the reader the difference between the historian and the historical novelist with regard to acts and actors is a qualitative one: the historian is preoccupied with 'historical' events, that is the kinds of event that seem crucial for a specific line of action to have unfolded the way it did, which in most cases means events of political significance involving primarily those in power, whereas the novelist, traditionally concerned with psychology and social relations on an everyday basis, will deal with events that seem minor or contingent from the historian's perspective.[5] This qualitative difference does not prevent the novelist from concerning himself with major 'historical' characters, but he has to stick to the general lines of historical 'truth' to maintain probability. The historian, on the other hand, trying to reconstruct and 'understand' a chain of events, thinks in terms of the causality and psychology well-known from fiction. Just as the novelist singles out one plot line from a limitless pool of potential plots and uses it at one and the same time as *terminus a quo* and *terminus ad quem* in his effort to make existence rational, the historian is apt to emphasize one line of events as more satisfactory than another to account for whatever historical complex he is studying. Both novelist and historian arrange their 'plots' by exclusion, because both want to make their discourses internally coherent. The historian knows his 'plot' before writing it in a way different from the way the novelist knows his. The novelist, at least if working along traditionally realistic lines, is very conscious of narrative efficiency, and to him the plot line must be assumed to have a high priority in the writing process. But to suggest that the historical discourse is a rendering into words of a purely chronological progression is to state an objective which in practice historians have never really aimed at. Historical accounts are seldom marked by strict adherence to the calendar. There are flash-backs and anticipations, there are alternations between emphasis on *temps* and *durée* as in literature. The aims may differ, but the technique and the effect on the reader, provided there is functional overlapping, remain identical. And a purely chronological progression would contradict the historian's declared aim of accounting for historical events. To proceed chronologically without consideration of causality would hardly amount to more than mere compilation of phenomena linked only on sequential conditions. Despite his familiar distinction between the two, E. M. Forster's definition of plot as time plus cause is as applicable to history as to fiction.[6] As finished products it is often hard to see the difference between the obviously teleological structure of the work of fiction and the explanatory efforts visible as the historian's comic or tragic cadences.

The *historical novelist* wants the reader to accept his narrative as more truthful than a text based on the 'dry' facts of history, claiming that the dramatic embellishments and conjecture produced by his novelistic imagination fill gaps in our knowledge of the past and make it come alive. The historical novel will endeavour to present a narrative universe which is both a textual continuum and in basic agreement with history. In conformity with the realistic novel, which provides the format for historical fiction, the historical novel invites reading attention to which the plausibility of its 'world' is unproblematic. As a historical text, which it also is, it must seem to offer information missing from the annals of history. In brief, the historical novel offers unity of narrative universe and complementarity with history. Since Scott the historical novel has been a species of narrative which exploits the possibilities of ready-made historical drama in conformity with the conventions of popular romance and realistic fiction. It supplies the facts of history, usually considered impersonal and dry, with human emotions and motivations, and it delights in filling in gaps in documentable fact, whether of the macrocosmic or the microcosmic kind. The essential qualification of the historical novelist is the ability to construct period pieces, and, in doing so, to allow full play to the illusion of the reality of the fictional universe.

The contemporary novelist experiments with his awareness of the historical in ways which differ from the traditional, usually romantic dramatization of famous figures and events sprinkled with a measure of more or less authentic social history. Whereas the historical novel fictionalizes history, imposing upon various bits and pieces of the past the totalizing perspective of the traditional novel, contemporary efforts to merge the historical with the fictional in the format of the novel seem to have had the exact opposite in view: problematizing the ability of 'meaningless' history to be transformed into the 'meaningful' novel. Instead of the historical novel we now tend to have 'historically conscious fiction,'[7] which invites the reader to appreciate problems related to ontology, epistemology, and discourse transformation. Among the more radical attempts at problematizing history and our historical awareness are John Fowles's *The French Lieutenant's Woman* from 1969 and, in a different thematic vein, Julian Barnes's *Flaubert's Parrot* from 1984, both of which simultaneously qualify as examples of what I elsewhere have dubbed 'documentary realism.'[8] In his much-discussed novel

Fowles makes a show of counterpointing the conventions of the historical novel with continual interruptions designed to demonstrate the precariousness of the historical perspective and the writer's inescapable situation in the time of writing, thus transforming the historical passages into pastiche. The demonstration takes the form of the persistent offering of the knowledge about the Victorian age available to the modern reader. In his novel about Flaubert, Barnes shows the impossibility of ever arriving at the truth about a real human being: the pieces in the jigsaw puzzle can be arranged in an infinite number of ways, according to the aims of the biographer. A telling example is the presentation of three alternative chronicles of Flaubert's life. One, by the relation of facts to that effect, gives the impression that he lived a happy and successful life; the second does the opposite; the third, comprising assorted quotations from Flaubert, shows us a disillusioned and frustrated, but above all – and this is evidently the point – a multi-facetted man.[9]

The metahistorical debate on the traditional, but problematic empirical claims of history, which has accelerated since the nineteen-sixties,[10] invites us to consider histories as texts sharing fundamental traits and assumptions with fictional texts (and also, for that matter, to make us re-appreciate historians' sources not as facts but as interpretations of facts), but it hardly makes us change our approach to history and fiction respectively. We may have become more aware that this or that historian draws considerably on traditional fictional patterns, but we do not suddenly want to mix the books from the shelves labelled 'fiction' and 'history.'

Readers look to biography in the hope of getting behind the official facades of more or less well-known figures of contemporary or historical interest. They want to know the real and entire story, with all the details, and they want a person's life to make some kind of overall sense. Of course the nature of the details varies enormously according to the kind and aim of the biography in question. There is an almost unbridgeable gap between on the one hand the gossip-saturated and scandal-mongering autobiography of the (in)famous Hollywood star, ghost-written by some unprincipled journalist who contributes to the glossy weeklies, and on the other the painstakingly researched scholarly monograph about a forgotten eighteenth-century politician with close attention to and scrupulous discussion of the tiniest and most un-sensational details. As regards sense-making, the common view is that the (auto)biographer should only transcribe the documented reality before him without trying to superimpose a pattern. But as any reader of biography knows, and as most writers of biography readily admit, the biographer is as much at pains to furnish a key to or a purpose for a person's life as the historian is to discover some dominant principle behind an apparently random collection of events.

With the possible exception of the most obstinate deconstructionist no one would deny an essential difference between a nonliterary text like the empirical historian's account and a literary text by an Updike or a Bellow, even though all of them seem to deal with the same kind of reality. But from the reader's perspective the difference is not due to any sense of a clearly demarcated distinction between fact and fiction in the text itself. Our impression of a difference has rather to do with differences between the potential uses or the applicability of the literary and the nonliterary texts respectively. To put it briefly, the literary text, by existing in a *metaphorical* relationship with the world in which the text is the vehicle and the world the tenor, is in principle ornamental. The nonliterary text, by existing in a *metonymical* relationship, is integral, that is, perceived to be part of our world. This does not mean that literature is unnecessary whereas nonliterature is necessary. Obviously we can, in a situation of enforced deprivation, do without either. The world will exist without the literary texts as it will without the nonliterary texts (not counting such texts as serve basically communicative functions): history books are just as superfluous as poems, even descriptions in learned journals are not needed to guarantee the event of the laboratory experiment. In relation to the world all texts are unnecessary, but this does not affect their different relationship with it. Just as the vehicle of the metaphor suggests a desired analogy to the tenor, expressing a wish to reinforce a feature already present in the tenor so that a hypothetical state of order results, literature departs from the world as we know it and takes us into a world where the analogy is in the reference to the phenomena of reality and the general wish expressed is the sense of an ending. In the nonliterary text no such state of analogy is desired. The nonliterary text replaces reality and in the process of doing so pretends to lose its textuality.

The reader's impression of looking through the nonliterary text at a nonlinguistic reality behind it establishes a perceived contrast between the literary text and the nonliterary text which is based not on feeling any difference between them in linguistic terms, but on sensing a difference between the literary as definitely a text – a book – and the nonliterary as a nontextual entity – an event, an experiment, nature, a character, etc. – not necessarily transcribable into text. This illusory difference in status between the literary and the nonliterary in terms of apparent textuality and nontextuality no doubt goes a long way to explaining why the literary text is so receptive and accommodating. The great illusion of the literary text resides precisely in its claim to represent the world in its nonliterary, that is its nontextual perspective. The literary text therefore welcomes any thematically relevant contribution from the 'real' world, because it is already potentially textual. Conversely the principle also explains the unwillingness of the nonliterary text to accommodate the literary, except, of course, as a source document. In relation to the nonliterary, supposedly nontextual, the literary always seems to be not only the imposition of an irresponsibly imaginative element – fiction as opposed to fact – but the imposition of the textual on the nontextual.

As a rule, literary histories are not exclusively histories of imaginative literature, encompassing as they do a wide variety of texts ranging from the classic literary genres of epic/fiction, poetry, and drama, through essays and letters, to regular historical sources. It has been suggested that it makes no sense to speak of 'literature' as synonymous with imaginative writing for three reasons: the lack of a definite number of necessary and sufficient elements shared by all literary works, the role played by readers' attitudes, and the unbroken continuum from the nonliterary to the literary.[11] The latitude conventionally accorded to literary inclusiveness is amply illustrated for example by the regularity with which literary histories mention works like Gibbon's *Decline and Fall of the Roman Empire* and Sir Winston Churchill's *History of the English Speaking Peoples,* or collections of essays (Hazlitt, Lamb, De Quincey, Eliot), letters (Paston, Chesterfield), or diaries (Pepys, Evelyn). In fact, the further we go back, the more inclusive does the sweep of modern literary historians become.[12]

Literature serves an existential function which cannot be put into a single formula, but which may provisionally – and hence somewhat crudely and provocatively – be characterized as unnecessary and complementary, in comparison with *work*, which in an existential perspective is necessary and essential. I am aware of a number of objections that may be raised from various perspectives against this simplification, quite apart from the obvious points that for a small group of people, including myself, reading literature is part of our job, and that for school children the same activity is an obligatory and sometimes onerous chore. It is customary for educators and critics to point to the desirability, even indispensability, of literature for the *Bildung* of mature human beings, and psychologists assert the value of literature in providing people with models to respond to, etc. But the fact remains that for a large number of people, literature – 'the world of books' – remains a luxury, something to be looked forward to and indulged in when one's daily duties have been fulfilled, and something which takes second place if more 'important' business must be attended to.[13]

If literature is existentially opposed to work, then it competes functionally with other kinds of leisure activities, and so must be distinguished from them in some other way. One distinction is between bookish and non-bookish activities: the competition is from all sorts of leisure activities ranging from games via excursions to drinking.[14] A further distinction can then be drawn between two basic kinds of bookish activities: informational vs. recreational reading. Some books such as language or science textbooks, however popularized, are distinctly providers of information (although the enjoyment they give may be identical with that experienced when reading recreationally), whereas the run-of-the-mill bestseller novel is distinctly recreational (although part of the trick in fiction of that kind is to make the reader feel he is being given valuable information[15]). The reader choosing to spend his free time reading a novel, or Gibbon's history, or Chesterfield's letters, knows full well that he has chosen an activity whose nature is determined not so much by any shared traits in the reading matter (although, of course, there are many) as by fulfilling a particular *function*. It would be convenient to have a single term covering the heterogeneous texts typically serving this specific purpose by a common name, and 'literature' may be conveniently and appropriately applied in this sense.

Although order may assume different guises, it is surely the narrative drive – a beginning promising a middle and an end consistent with it – which has the strongest force. Literature relying on narrative efficiency – fascination-potential and suspense – is central to the function of recreational reading.[16] The unity endowed by a strong narrative line determines the degree to which the text can satisfy the literary function. If the metonymy provided by the plot gives place to the metaphoric principle, as in much modernist fiction, the narrative-expecting reader will find it harder to naturalize his experience of the text. Paradoxically, strongly metaphorical literature like the modernist and postmodernist novel or lyrical poetry, may often be felt to yield satisfaction only if approached via the purely informational function. If the metonymies get out of hand, as in reference-ridden histories, interest will probably again slacken, and the reader will feel a shift in function. Plot-heavy fiction like the thriller has pride of place when it comes to narrative priority. In no other kind of fiction are all other elements subordinated to such a high degree to the requirements of the plot. From the historical novel there is a smooth transition to the popular history, and from the psychological novel there is an equally smooth transition to the biography. In both cases the shift in function from the recreational to the informational may occur if the intrinsic-ordering principle is felt to be too weak.

The operative value of a distinction between the more inclusive 'literature' and the less inclusive 'fiction' seems highly questionable in a functional perspective. It may even be the case that readers have an awareness of specific literary genres rather than an awareness of a distinction between categories on the comparatively high level of abstraction where we talk about 'literature' and 'fiction,' however logical the status of the second may be in comparison with the first.

It would indeed be very difficult to find prose texts which cannot be shown to have the verbal traits characteristic of narrative fiction. History and biography (the latter perhaps the form of nonfictional narrative closest to fiction because of its focus on an individual in a morally, financially, and erotically influential environment), informal essays, and reportage, all frequently have the narrative qualities which make for 'a good read.' All kinds of text have the potential for being responded to in terms of literature, thanks to our craving to endow the baffling confusion of an apparently meaningless existence with a coherent framework and a sense of direction. The metaphorics of the news industry continuously manifests this potential, which it is itself so busy recreating. It has long since become a convention that news is served to readers and viewers as 'stories,' that the journalist is in search of a 'good story,' etc. Indeed, any text with a claim to communicative efficiency makes use of basic narrative devices shared by fiction, so narrative structure is hardly the level of analysis at which we should look for a distinction.

The urge in the biography to get at the reality beneath the surface and to discover a unity in a life is not very different from the urge in the novel to tell the 'real' story with all the details and to subordinate a fictional universe to a thematic idea. No doubt the similarity of the biography to the realistic novel regarding detail and sense-making goes a long way to explain its popularity in the wider public of fiction-readers. Indeed, it can be very difficult to draw sharp distinctions between certain kinds of history like biography and fiction. Starting at one end with Richard Ellman's lives of Joyce and Wilde, it is possible to progress along an increasingly fictionalising axis via Michael Holroyd's noteless but still scholarly biography of Shaw and the decidedly literary biography of Shelley by Maurois, on to instances in which the boundary to fiction proper has been just transgressed, as in Irving Stone's *The Passions of the Mind* or Carey Harrison's *Freud. A Novel*, and still further to more radically literary experimentation as in Thomas's Freud fiction *The White Hotel*.[17] At the opposite extreme from the scholarly biography we find fiction in which biography and biographical method are transformed into metafictional problematization, as in Julian Barnes's *Flaubert's Parrot*. A consequence of applying the functional perspective is the need to accept the lack of any permanent status for a given text. It becomes a free agent to be categorized only by the reader's functionally determined response to it. At either end of the range there are, of course, texts which, under normal circumstances, will tolerate only one functional use. But as we move towards the fictional from the historical, a dual function appears at the point where conventionally literary characteristics begin to become appreciable.

Whereas all kinds of text which from a generic perspective are non-literary have the potential to acquire literary status when viewed from a functional perspective, this is not the case with regard to change of status in the opposite direction, when literary texts are used as source material in cultural and historical studies, or as elements in various kinds of persuasive discourses such as the political speech or the newspaper advertisement. For literary function as distinct from other textual functions, the most important of which are the informational and the rhetorical/affective/propagandistic, depends on the attitude of the reader in the moment of reading. If fulfilling a predominantly recreational function even informational and rhetorical texts may be read as literature, and *vice versa*, for instance when the literary text is read by the social historian. But certain kinds of text are felt to be essentially literary, and if fulfilling any other function, they seem to be exploited for alien purposes. The availability of elements characteristic of texts aimed at fulfilling the literary function makes it possible for a writer to 'program' his text to invite a response in terms of literary function. At times lying readily to hand virtually as a kit of literary tools – like the neoclassical poet's poetic diction – and nowadays often thought of as a cumulative store of the nuts and bolts of literary mechanics, to be collected in glossaries and manuals of critical concepts and terms ready to be taught to classes of students eager to learn about the workings of literature, 'literariness' widely enjoys the status of a linguistic option or a communicative register. The writer can draw on these conventions, follow them or rebel against them, and so make clear his *intention* that his text should perform in a literary function. This application of certain linguistic elements, both intrinsically to make up the text's particular imaginative quality, and in a meta-communicational code system carrying a message about the writer's intention, may sometimes be reinforced by factors outside the writer's control. The publisher who promotes a historical work as being 'as exciting as a novel,' deliberately intends to influence a potential reader's functional categorization of the work, in this case of course in the fond hope that appeal to the craving for recreation as well as the appetite for information will make the work sell better.

Roughly speaking there are four determinants for the reader's categorization of a given text: style, that is certain linguistic conventions; intention (ranging from text-intrinsic declarations by the author to advertising hype); context and function. The four determinants obviously work together in a system of presupposition. The declaration of intention by the writer presupposes some degree of familiarity with textual categorization on the part of the reader, which is further helped along with considerations about context and style, which in turn make sense only against a background of clarified function, and so on. It would be futile to embark on a quest for first causes. As soon as a small child has heard its first story, it is potentially aware of certain markers of style ('Once upon a time…'), intention ('Now I'll tell you a *story*'), context ('Tell me *another* story, do!'), and function ('I'll tell you a *bedtime* story'). This potential awareness may become actualized if the necessity of making distinctions arises, but most of the time the awareness is probably actualised only to the level at which the reader calls on experience to attune his mind to factual or fictional text. The awareness lies dormant if a regular routine is followed, but is awakened in case of deviation. Most readers would nod in recognition to a day starting with breakfast and a newspaper, followed by a period of work during which the consultation of various kinds of written material is indispensable, and then, on getting home and having seen to the household duties, relaxation with a book. And there is no change in principle if for printed material we substitute the 'texts' offered by the electronic media.[18] What would disturb the reader/viewer/listener would be a breach in the conventions followed in the texts: if, for instance, the breakfast newspaper or the morning news on the radio suddenly presented a short story, or if the book or film enjoyed for relaxation in the evening turns out to be a purely instructional text.

The metafictional and documentary devices so popular in postmodernist fiction derive their effect from thwarting familiar expectations. What happens in the reading of metafiction, documentary realism, and nonfiction 'fiction' is that the reader is invited or obliged to re-align his bearings by contextualizations different from those of traditional realistic fiction. In the case of metafiction the fictional text becomes indistinguishable from its critical reading, because the two are inextricably woven together. In the cases of documentary realism and nonfiction fiction the contexts are the nonfictional, indeed antifictional areas where the documentary has first priority, from the historical treatise to the TV news program.

David Lodge's description of fiction as an open category suggests that a text is accepted as fictional as long as it does not violate the reader's established expectations of what the fictional is like.[19] This argument is tacitly based on the verbal similarity of fictional and nonfictional discourses. But the supposition that there is really no linguistically appreciable difference between the kind of expository prose employed to communicate facts on the one hand and imaginative constructs on the other is hardly a new one. The utterance 'In 1902 Father built a house at the crest of the Broadview Avenue Hill in New Rochelle, New York' reads like what in J. L. Austin's terminology is called a constative statement: it may be pronounced true or false (1970). But as the utterance appears as the first sentence in a book announced unambiguously as a novel (E. L. Doctorow's *Ragtime*), the literary response entails shifting the significance of the utterance from the constative to the performative, still in Austin's terminology.[20] The performative function of creating the event by stating it does not negate the historical truth or falsehood of the statement, but the relevance of the constative import, in consequence of being overridden by the performative, is shifted from referentiality – its being true or false – to consistency; a consistency which nonetheless, as regards realistic writing, must always display an awareness of its referential potential. The function of a given statement, however constative, will always be transformed into a performative one, whenever the text invites categorization as literary rather than historical. Likewise a performative statement will be accepted as a constative one if the context invites categorization as factual, a circumstance to which the standard accusation against historians for subjectivity bears ample witness. The structure that indicates the fictionality of a text or enables it to be read as if it were fictional is, in the case of realistic fiction, either a structure sharing the assumption of fidelity or at least probability in the representation of experiential reality, or a structure displaying one or more conventional linguistical markers of the fictional discourse. The reader's acceptance of realism does not so much depend on the suspense of disbelief as on his not being prompted to disbelief by too blatant a defiance of a probability based on possibility.

A sentence like the one quoted from Doctorow therefore does not defy categorization as a performative statement and will confirm expectations of realistic fiction, because its environment – blurb description, etc. – signals prose fiction, even though there is nothing in the syntax or morphology which is literary *per se*.[21] However, fiction does make use of certain linguistic conventions which have become accepted as signals of a certain verbal function. The poetic diction of Neoclassical poetry is a textbook example of a highly refined but also rigoristically one-purpose *langue* – within – the – *langue*. In the opening sentence from *Ragtime* the word 'Father' is the verbal element that stands out from the rest of the sentence indicating a degree of intimacy between narrator and narratee not conventional in 'neutral' expository prose, but well within the horizon of verbal expectations in memoirs and – bearing in mind the essentially hybrid nature of the realistic novel – in the fictional convention which has integrated that nonfictional genre. Among such verbal fiction markers are a range of stylistic mannerisms. As illustrated in the Doctorow sentence they are not inherently fictional, but associated with fiction because fiction has long since put its stamp on a variety of styles not specifically literary.[22] In her study of autobiography Elizabeth W. Bruss suggests 'some linguistic markers sensitive to context,' which are verbal areas where the autobiographer will be likely to genre-stamp his discourse.[23] In the same manner it is possible to point to similar context-sensitive markers signalling the literary, from the stereotypes of obsolescent poetic diction through conventional prose-narrative techniques to the verbal ironies of modernist poetry and the narrative conventions of metafiction. In the case of the realistic novel such markers would include discourse in the perspective of its state of report (typically free indirect speech), deixis (the conventional trick of assuming familiarity by using the definite article without an introductory indefinite article), and aspect (using the simple past where otherwise the expanded past would have been the grammatical rule[24]). Such verbal conventions, however, are not linguistically unique to the fictional text, but may be used in verbal communications with other functions. The problem is well illustrated by the way Jakobson asks what is the empirical, linguistic criterion of the poetic function, assuming that a specific verbal pattern gives rise to a communicative function, and not vice versa.[25]

But a text, or more typically brief passages in a text, may be poetic without this affecting the general, non-poetic function of the text.[26] Advertising and sports journalism are two non-fictional types of communication that come to mind in this connection. We do not classify a reportage from a football match as poetry, although it often contains quantities of – admittedly more or less stereotyped – tropes. Neither do we wish to read as poetry a newspaper or TV advertisement, despite the fact that such communications very often build on a dominant metaphor. Language itself, despite Jakobson's notion of the poetic as the projection of the principle of equivalence from the axis of selection into the axis of combination, is not enough to establish poetic function, because intention, context, or function (not, however, in the narrow sense used by Jakobson) individually or together may render a poetic 'deciphering' irrelevant or at best instrumental only. Undoubtedly readers preparing to read a book subtitled *Collected Poems* will be likely to accept readily the verbal constructs in a poetic function no matter how referential, prosaic, and trope-free the contents of the volume turn out to be; and the historian employing a number of metaphors to enliven his account or perhaps making use of a dominating metaphor that he finds apt for his argument, will hardly be considered a traitor to his profession.[27]

The degree to which an exclusively linguistic principle, like Jakobson's projection-of-equivalence, can be said to determine the nature of a given text as literary, depends on the emphasis with which it is foregrounded in the text and the preparedness and/or willingness of the audience to accept the text as a whole as literary. This last condition is quite in agreement with the two 'infelicities' that Austin detects in the performative statement. For such a statement to work the first condition is that 'the convention invoked must exist and be accepted.'[28] The second condition is that 'the circumstances in which we purport to invoke this procedure must be appropriate for its invocation.'[29] This is to combine conditions of context and function. To read the marriage rite as literature would obviously not do to complete a wedding ceremony. To read fiction for its informative value would be sensible only to a certain point. But to read an informative text as literature is perfectly feasible, and it is this principle that the historical novel relies on.

Since Wimsatt and Beardsley delivered their crushing blow to the validity of intention as an interpretative avenue, the concept has led a precarious existence in literary criticism.[30] Despite strong reactions against such New-Critical tenets as textual autonomy, textual unity through verbal tension, etc., the mistrust of intention seems to have lingered on in the critical schools outside those relying imperturbably on the biographical approach.[31] From a reader's perspective, however, in order better to appreciate the notion of category which is an integral element of reading, it makes good sense not only to retain the concept of intention but to extend its meaning beyond strictly authorial intention to encompass a complex of supplementary, even sometimes overriding, markers. Some of them form part of the discourse, for instance the narrator's comments; some of them are part of the volume in hand, typically expressed in the blurb text and the hype advertising quoted; some of them are part of a larger context ranging from authorial remarks not directly bearing on the text under consideration to the implicit intentionality 'programming' of genre.

It is hardly possible to distinguish between intention and context in this extended sense of the former. Rather, the two categories seem aspects of one another. Any statement about intention – text-internal or text-external – will be valid only in relation to a system of conventions, typically in the acceptance or rejection of them. Jonathan Culler has suggestively demonstrated the degree to which a given text is naturalized by the 'competent' reader in terms of context.[32] The naturalization can also be seen, however, as a dynamics of comparing markers of intention with the reader's textual experience. We may take Oscar Lewis's *The Children of Sanchez* as an example.

In the 1940s and 1950s Professor Lewis carried out anthropological field work in Mexico. Much of his work consisted of tape-recording interviews with various population groups. The interview material collected from a specific family he decided to publish virtually unprocessed as a series of case histories speaking for themselves as *The Children of Sanchez* in 1961. To most readers in the part of the world serviced by Penguin Books his collection of taped interviews was made accessible as a paperback (first published 1964) in the series 'Penguin Modern Classics.' For the reader unaware of the history and nature of the book it may come as something of a surprise that it is actually not a work of fiction. The information offered on the back cover, the usual mixture of quotation from positive criticism and the publisher's own paraphrase-cum-hype, serves the function of meeting affirmatively the reader's expectation of just another novel. The happy-ending quality of the average sentimental light novel is implicit in an excerpt from Stuart Hampshire's review in *Twentieth Century*: ' "The most vivid, complete, and internal description of modern poverty, and of the survival of poverty, that I have ever read."' In the concluding quotation the *Times Literary Supplement* reviewer comes as close to fictional categorization as possible: 'Has the quality of a great novel... No doubt each expert will take his picking. But for the general reader it will, like all other true works of art, speak only for itself.'" (Deletion as quoted.) In between the blurb writer has managed to shape a smooth transition from Stuart Hampshire's suggestion of the fictional quality of Lewis's book to the *TLS* adoption of that view: '...this rare work stands like a monument at the point where literature meets life. One cannot help admiring the artistry with which Professor Oscar Lewis has cut and edited living speech into a work of art.' For the reader not especially interested in or well-informed about anthropology, the publisher's obvious intention to steer reader expectations away from the nonfictionality of science in the direction of the fictionality of the novel will result in an automatic shift of context within which to naturalize the text. It may well be the case that *The Children of Sanchez* will reach a larger public as a quasi-novel, but at the same time it may be feared that the publisher's promotional presentation on a basis of fictionality may undermine the author's somewhat concealed intention as expressed towards the end of his introduction – the sort of long and apparently tedious introduction that 'classics' will often be issued with and which are supposedly often skipped by the reader eager to begin the real story – to urge reconsideration of the way aid should be given to under-developed countries. It is indeed possible to argue that once the reader has accepted the intentional (re)direction on the back cover, such a nonfictional marker as the subtitle 'Autobiography of a Mexican Family' on the title page serves to contextualize the text as fiction according to the convention that the very proof of the fictionality of a narrative is in its insistence on its own factual nature. The reader approaching Professor Lewis's book as a work of fiction will, as demonstrated persuasively by Michal Glowinsky,[33] find his expectations confirmed by the obviously fictional structuring of the work, and even if he reads about the factual background in the introduction, will probably soon forget this request for nonfictional contextualization.

The Children of Sanchez shows not only how text-external endeavours to secure naturalization in a specific kind of context work with great force to determine the reader's overall approach, but also how a clash of intentions within the work itself – introduction versus structuration – is subject to arbitration in terms of context conventions.

Intention invoking context and context signalling intention are forceful determinants for the reader's functional categorization of a given text. The dynamics of the intention-context complex for the functional assignment in the example of the Penguin edition of *The Children of Sanchez* illustrates a tendency, obviously in the interest of publishers wishing their specialised publications to reach a larger reading public, not so much to change nonfiction into fiction, as to deflect a reader response through inviting a revised functional acceptance. If the tendency to assign a literary function to nonfictional texts has been much enhanced by the sharp division of our modern existence into work and leisure and by the increasingly visible part played by the entertainment element in all kinds of mass communications, the opposite tendency, that is the invitation to consider the text signalled as literary in a nonliterary function, seems to be of a less clearcut nature. Since the earliest times writers and critics have insisted on the combined pleasure and usefulness of literature, so assignment to the nonliterary function has always been felt as part of the response proper to literature. The deliberate re-assignment of functional categories is seen in literature with a declared didactic aim, but surely the morally or politically improving potential of didactic literature is of a nature different from what we mean by the 'useful' function of, for instance, the historical text. A shift from the literary to the nonliterary functional category, in the reverse of the manner of *The Children of Sanchez*, seems to apply only in cases where a literary text is made into source or background documentation for the historian, for instance as a particularly precise description of a political climate. Daniel Defoe's *Robinson Crusoe* is an excellent demonstration of the *homo capitalisticus* of the early eighteenth century, and Restoration drama with its detailed representation of the late-seventeenth-century ethos of the English court is often referred to by the social historian.

The difference between the work of fiction and the work of history is, at the best of times, a difficult one to assess. Traditionally we say that historians deal with 'hard' facts, creative writers with 'human' truth. But, as argued above, it is not so much the text *qua* text which possesses a certain relationship with 'reality' at any given time. In the last instance what seems to count is the impact of what the written has on our making sense of existence. Instead of suggesting categorical ideas and general notions we ought perhaps to consider instead what particular purposes and functions are served by individual texts, but always with a keen eye on their specifically explicitly and implicitly contextual and functional claims.

Notes

1. Julian Barnes, *Flaubert's Parrot* (London: Jonathan Cape, 1984). Here quoted from the 1985 Picador paperback edition, p. 14.
2. Ibid., p. 38.
3. Cp. Dominick LaCapra's dicta that: 'documents are texts that supplement or rework "reality" and not mere sources that divulge facts about "reality"' (Dominick LaCapra, *History and Criticism*. [Ithaca and London: Cornell University Press, 1985], p. 11), and '"documents" are themselves texts that "process" or rework "reality" and require a critical reading that goes beyond traditional philological forms of *Quellenkritik*' (LaCapra, ibid., pp. 19-20). About the chronicle and the annal in particular, as distinct from the history proper, Hayden White suggests that they should be approached as 'particular products of possible conceptions of historical reality, conceptions that are alternatives to, rather than failed anticipations of, the fully realized historical discourse that the modern history form is supposed to embody' (Hayden White, 'The Value of Narrativity in the Representation of Reality,' *Critical Inquiry*, 7, 1980, p. 10).
4. It may have been with this development in mind that Tom Stoppard devised a deliberately stylized scenario for his TV drama documentary on the budding Solidarity movement in Poland *Squaring the Circle* (London: Faber, 1984).
5. Cp. E. H. Carr's equation of propaganda and the historical novel, because both genres 'merely use facts of the past to embroider a kind of writing which has nothing to do with history' (E. H. Carr, *What is History?* [Harmondsworth: Penguin, 1987 (orig. publ. 1961)], p. 29).

6. Cp. Hayden White on the characteristics of the historical account, which ends in a 'postmodernist' paraphrase of Forster: 'But by common consent, it is not enough that a historical account deal in real, rather than merely imaginary, events; and it is not enough that the account in its order of discourse represent events according to the chronological sequence in which they originally occurred. The events must be not only registered within the chronological framework of their original occurrence but narrated as well, that is to say, revealed as possessing a structure, an order of meaning, which they do *not* possess as mere sequence' (White, op.cit., p. 9 [White's italics]).
7. Cp. e.g. B. Foley, 'From *U.S.A.* to *Ragtime*: Notes on the Forms of Historical Consciousness in Modern Fiction,' *American Literature*, 50, 1, March, 1978, p. 86.
8. Cp. my study *Fact into Fiction: Documentary Realism in the Contemporary Novel* (London: Macmillan; New York: St. Martin's Press, 1991), in which I attempt to identify a mode of writing which embeds documentary texts and references significantly in the fiction.
9. Op. cit., pp. 23-37.
10. Probably because the problematic difference between history and story has been a matter of constant worry to historians eager to maintain their 'science' on an empirical basis. Since the nineteen-sixties meta-historical issues have been claiming increasing attention, and the debate in general in the field has been centered on the relationship between 'objective' historiography and 'subjective' imaginative literature, to a considerable extent inspired by the concepts of structuralist and post-structuralist literary theory.
11. J. R. Searle's objection to the usefulness of 'literature' for the discussion of fictionality is based on what he calls the logical status of the fictional discourse, a status which derives from the opposition between fictional and serious utterances in general. In the pragmatic perspective of function, however, the concept of literature makes sense despite the blurred contours it may reveal when exposed to generic, linguistic, or epistemological analysis. In the functional perspective, Searle's distinction between fictionality and seriousness is neutralized, since the reader does not engage in a contract with reality through the book, but agrees initially that the literary experience requires the suspension of disbelief. It is a very strong urge in recreational reading be it of fictional ('serious' or 'light') or nonfictional literature, to see one's expectations of order met with. (J. R. Searle, 'The Logical Status of Fictional Discourse,' *New Literary History*, 6, 2, Winter 1975, 319-32.)
12. For the purposes of the present discussion I ignore the use of 'literary' as a qualitative term given to especially 'well-written' nonfictional works.
13. It will be noted that I am arguing in a dimension much more concrete than the one represented by, for instance, D. H. Lawrence when he suggests that the 'essential function of art is moral. Not aesthetic, not decorative, not pastime and recreation. But moral. The essential function of art is moral' (D. H. Lawrence, *Studies in Classic American Literature*. [Harmondsworth: Penguin, 1971 (orig. publ. 1924)], p. 180).

14. In *Britain in Figures*, for example, reading appears on a list with the following competing leisure activities: television, crafts and hobbies, gardening, physical recreation, social activities, decorating and house/vehicle maintenance, excursions, park visits and walks, games and club activities, drinking (A. F. Sillitoe, A. F. *Britain in Figures* [Harmondsworth: Penguin, 1971], p. 65).
15. James A. Michener, Arthur Hailey, Harold Robbins, and Morris L. West would be representative.
16. Fascination potential is of two kinds: extrinsic and intrinsic. Certain topics, as the writers of bestsellers know, are almost automatically fascinating. But fascination, that is the power of a text to hook and keep the reader hooked, is also a matter of the writer's ability to keep the reader's interest alive by devices ranging from stylistic and thematic interest to the comparatively crude forms of suspense, which is, as suggested by A. J. Greimas in 1966 (*Semantique Structurale* [Paris: Librarie Larousse]), basically a matter of keeping elements which logically belong together at a distance from each other.
17. C. Harrison, *Freud: A Novel*. (Harmondsworth: Penguin, 1984). I. Stone,*The Passions of the Mind* (London: Cassell, 1971). D. M. Thomas, *The White Hotel* (London: Gollancz, 1981).
18. Largely due to the efforts of semioticians since the early sixties, the theoretical barriers between the different media have been broken down so that we now are dealing, willy-nilly, with one large complex of texts, understood as a system of signification and approachable according to the model of linguistics. It therefore seems almost heretical when Peter Faulkner stubbornly insists on a qualitative difference: 'The written word, which can be considered again and again, is a medium which particularly challenges rational scrutiny and develops individual discrimination. The much more direct emotive power of music and the visual arts makes them more appropriate to the various forms of ritual which liberate the individual from his burden of self-consciousness – but at the cost, which the humanist is not prepared to pay, of the withdrawal from responsibility for his own life and fate' (P. Faulkner, *Humanism in the English Novel* [London: Pemberton, 1975], p. 192).
19. Cp. D. Lodge, *The Modes of Modern Writing: Metaphor, Metonymy, and the Typology of Modern Literature* (London: Longman, 1977).
20. '*Ragtime* began with a description of his house in New Rochelle' (P. Levine, *Contemporary Writers: E. L. Doctorow* [London and New York: Macmillan, 1975], p. 78).
21. Of course the autobiography cannot be ruled out by the utterance alone, but only by the signals from the printed environment.
22. Cp. Bakhtin as summarised by Dominick LaCapra: 'for Bakhtin the novel was a genre that tested the limits of generic classification and continually renewed itself by incorporating other genres and social usages in an active interchange of perspective and voices' (op.cit., p. 116).
23. The areas are: Person or title, space (indicators), tense and aspect, modality, mood, reported speech, performatives (indicators of narrative stance), case,

and focus, (Bruss, E. W., *Autobiographical Acts: The Changing Situation of a Literary Genre.* [Baltimore and London: Johns Hopkins University Press, 1976], pp. 31-2).
24. Cp. C. Bache, 'Tense and Aspect in Fiction', *Journal of Literary Semantics,* 15, 2, 1986, 82-97, on aspectual differences relating to fictional and nonfictional narrative.
25. R. Jakobson, 'Closing Statement: Linguistics and Poetry.' *Style in Language,* ed. Thomas A. Sebeok (Cambridge, Ms.: Cambridge Technology Press of Massachusettes, 1960 [orig. publ. 1958]).
26. Cp. Searle, op. cit., on the figurative and the literal.
27. I shall not go further into a detailed discussion of the intricate linguistic problems, but only, as an example of the non-exclusiveness of such allegedly linguistic markers of fiction, point to the fact that the aspect characteristic of fiction suggested in Bache op.cit. seems to be indicative of a much larger category, what may be called the narrative register, characterized by being an account after the 'event,' whether factual or fictional.
28. J. L. Austin, 'Performative Utterances' in *Philosophical Papers* (Oxford: Oxford University Press, 1970 [orig. publ. 1956]), p. 237.
29. Ibid.
30. Wimsatt and Beardsley, 'The Intentional Fallacy' in *The Verbal Icon: Studies in the Meaning of Poetry* (Lexington, Kentucky: University of Kentucky Press, 1954).
31. Despite Wimsatt and Beardsley and their successors, biographical criticism inside as well as outside academe has been and still is a thriving, indeed lucrative business.
32. J. Culler, *Structuralist Poetics: Structuralism, Linguistics and the Study of Literature* (London: Routledge and Kegan Paul Ltd., 1975).
33. Glowinski, M. (1987). 'Document as Novel,' *New Literary History,* 18 Winter, 385-401.

The historical turn is coming – and it's about time, too!

Jens Rahbek Rasmussen

"Postmodernists' primary goal has been to challenge convictions about the objectivity of knowledge and the stability of language", thereby questioning the belief in progress and "the individual as knower and doer", wrote three American historians a few years ago. Noting that postmodernist critics of history seemed to "operate in the attack mode", their own goal was to defend "the role of an objective and inclusive history while recognizing the need for exploring its conceptual fault lines."[1] Another book which attempted more or less the same task some years later was given the title *In defence of history*.[2]

So historians feel besieged – again. They never seem to be able to do anything right. Around 1900 history as a discipline suffered from an inferiority complex vis-a-vis science (i.e. the exact and natural sciences); around 1950 the same applied in relation to the social sciences. In 1900 historians resigned themselves to be unscientific; in 1950 many were willing to accept the humble position as suppliers of facts to sociology and other generalizing disciplines. Some did try to make their work more like the social sciences, like the *Annales* school in France and the American "cliometricians", but were soon told that this was an unnatural aberration; historians should tell stories, and "the revival of narrative" was much heralded c. 1980.

But then came the "postmodernist challenge", or "the linguistic turn", or "the triumph of Theory" – take your pick. The opening quote will have given an idea of what that was about. Another historian, who was a good deal more sympathetic to these trends, nevertheless described them in fairly similar terms:

[They stressed] language, meaning, and interpretation as central to human understanding and therefore to understanding humans. [They asserted] that the methodologies and knowledge embodied in scholarly disciplines were not universal and timeless but socially and culturally constituted... [They] questioned the very dichotomies that grounded the paradigm of traditional history: the supposedly inherent differences between literature and science, reality and its representations...[they] repudiated the unified and usually omniscient viewpoint of traditional history-telling in favor of diversity of gender, race, ethnicity, and other social distinctions."[3]

Now much of this was perhaps not too far from the actual practice of historians, but then this was the "weak" variety. There soon developed a "strong" variety which in effect dismissed the concept of an objective reality, recognized little difference between fact and fiction, and argued that "all the world is a text". In almost Mao-like slogans, the weak version said: "Resist authority" – that is, the traditional history dominated by white elite males should be challenged by viewpoints relating to class, gender, race etc. The strong version said: "Question reality", and this is where historians started getting nervous – the more so as it soon became apparent that the relevant question could really only be answered in the negative. If all you could do was to play language games, why have historians at all? Why not sack the lot and have them replaced with people properly trained in analyzing (or deconstructing) texts – "textualists" rather than "contextualists". You might forgive historians for thinking that they were being told to get lost. Accepting the new ideas seemed a little like turkeys voting for Christmas.[4]

In fact one Danish deconstructionist, Hans Hauge, explicitly declared historians redundant.[5] After all they were nothing but "naive believers" in reality, claiming to be capable of "representing" the past. But what they actually produced was not only indistinguishable from fiction, it was outdated fiction: historians had stuck to realism, whereas literature had succeeded in moving on to modernism (and presumably beyond that to postmodernism, though he did not specify this). Historians could not however admit that they were "really" writing literature, because that would challenge the idea of history as an academic discipline. Hauge therefore suggested that all departments of history be dissolved and the study of history transferred to other departments – presumably those of language and literature.

Historians have reacted variously to the new ideas. Some react angrily and dismiss either all theory (Windschuttle) or at least all cultural/linguistic theory (Palmer); others try to sift the useful from the useless (Appleby et al., Evans). Or as an American historian, Geoff Eley, puts it: a few have gone all the way "through the terrain of textuality to the land of discourse and deconstruction"; a much larger group "continues much as before, generally aware of what is happening but uninterested in the theory behind the linguistic turn and essentially wishing that it would go away. And then there are the rest of us, partly there for the ride, partly curious to see where it goes, and not at all sure we'll stay very long at the destination."[6]

Surprisingly what would seem the most obvious counter-argument – to provide a historical explanation of the rise of postmodernism – was left to non-historians.[7] The American marxist critic Fredric Jameson argued that "the transformation of reality into signs and texts occurs necessarily in a society that values consumerism… a strong textualist program of representational analysis reinforces the logic of consumer capitalism as it reproduces it." History "is transmuted into a series of perpetual presents as synchronic analysis is substituted for the dynamics of diachronic analysis". Or in another version: "Market capitalism begat realism; monopoly capitalism begat modernism; and therefore multinational capitalism begets postmodernism." Still others noticed that the "claim that verbal constructs do not correspond in a direct way to reality" arose among elite white males exactly when "women and non-Western people have begun to speak for themselves, and, indeed, to speak about global power differentials".[8]

For, as Berkhofer reluctantly concedes, you have two paradigms competing: the postmodern (textualist) and the mainstream (contextualist). Proponents of the latter

> contextualize their textualist opponents according to their own ideology of realism, which purports to know that their constructed context corresponds to the real world. They claim, in other words, that they can operate outside the postmodernist universe of hegemonic discourse that they argue textualists inhabit.

In other words: you either subscribe to the "ideology of realism" or to the "ideology of language". In both cases you can argue coherently that the opposing view is nonsense, but you are unlikely to convince your opponents, because they do not accept the basic premisses of the argument.

Postmodernism is difficult to define, though usually easy enough to recognize, not least in the use of "theory" (which even its proponents admit is difficult to specify).[9] Its influence has been strongest in literary and cultural studies, though it has also had an effect, not only in history, but also in perhaps more unlikely disciplines such as law, geography and management. On the one hand it is based on the fluidity and indeterminacy of language, and characterized by paradox and playfulness; on the other hand its claims are advanced as undeniably true. If you challenge "theory" you must be either slow-witted or a conservative out to defend academic power (which sits oddly with the obvious attempt to make "theory" the new key discipline for all arts and humanities).

Thus any real debate is impossible. It certainly does not help that "theory" is invariably couched in deliberately obscure prose (obscurity signalling profundity), whereas readable prose and clarity in presentation are seen as the "conceptual tools of conservatism."[10] Because it is so (needlessly) difficult, students are reluctant to admit that much of it is hot air. Only insiders can criticize "theory", but having invested many years of hard work to master it, they are unlikely to do so.

The way in which postmodernism has managed to establish itself as a master science, itself exempt from the criticism it subjects others to, is strongly reminiscent of the role of marxism in the 1970's. As the historian Eric Hobsbawm once put it, being a marxist in the 1950's had its problems, but at least one advantage: without an uncritical audience of like-minded colleagues and students, you had to convince people who were initially sceptical that your interpretation was valid. When such an uncritical audience was created, all kinds of jargon and gibberish emerged. Watching postmodernism in the 1990's gives you an eerie feeling of *déja-vu*. Indeed there are more similarities between the academic strategies of the two movements than either of them is probably comfortable with – down to the use of phrases like "it is no accident that...", when it is only too evident that that is precisely what it is.

Several works have pointed out that the philosophical premisses of postmodernism, far from being obviously true, or new, are in fact well-known and hotly contested (to use a postmodernist buzzword).[11] Throughout the history of philosophy there has been this opposition between on the one hand anti-realism, relativism and critique of objectivity, and on the other realism or "common sense".[12]

Although there are certainly shortcomings enough to be found in postmodernism's "home ground", literary and cultural studies, its weaknesses become especially glaring once it moves outside this turf. This was demonstrated when an American physicist, Alan Sokal, submitted a spoof article – with liberal quotes from postmodernists pontificating about science – to the journal *Social Text*, and had it accepted.[13] But the same near-total ignorance applies to debates about history. My favourite example is the following rebuke from a postmodernist sympathizer to mainstream historians:

> Historical knowledge works by posing, re-posing and displacing questions, *not* by accumulating 'evidence' independently of them. Facts are not given, it is only relative to a question that we can begin to assess the value of those materials which are to constitute evidence for the answer to it.[14]

Now in my view it would be difficult to find a more *unexceptional* statement, something which better expressed precisely the viewpoint of *mainstream* historians; but then admittedly we are here far from the "strong" postmodernist scepticism and relativism.[15] The gap between "strong" postmodernism and what they imagine historians are up to seems indeed unbridgable; that between the "weak" version and real-life historiography is not.

The Danish debate has focussed on Hayden White's *Metahistory* from 1973.[16] White pointed out that historians use various narrative and rhetorical conventions so that the events they wrote about are given a spurious coherence and even a moral or allegorical meaning; and he seemed to say that history, being governed by such narrative conventions, was therefore indistinguishable from fiction, and that it was impossible to "privilege" one historical interpretation over another.[17] Confronted with the question whether that applied to "revisionist" interpretations as well (which deny the Nazi genocide of Jews), White seemed to modify his position. That same question led another scholar, Lionel Gossman, to retract his former views (fairly similar to White's); Gossman now emphasizes the need to distinguish between history and fiction and to avoid a "facile and irresponsible relativism".[18] White's basic argument – history and fiction both employ narrative, so history must be fiction – has also been comprehensively refuted by narratologists.[19] (Of course this does not imply that e.g. historical novels, films etc. cannot play an important role in the communication of history. Most historians would readily concede that novelists can reach a deeper "truth" than historians, restricted by their sources.)[20]

Historians have generally been sceptical about blurring the difference between genres, as shown by the debate around Simon Schama's *Dead certainties*.[21] In his account of the battle at Quebec 1759 Schama (among other material) used a letter purporting to be an eyewitness account from a soldier in that battle, but which was in fact by Schama himself (as his afterword made clear). This did not go well with most of his colleagues, though surely the important thing is that Schama was fully aware of what he was doing and told his readers about it.[22]

But of course such experiments do not necessarily have greater appeal than traditional stuff, as Berkhofer admits: "To convey an explicit radical political message effectively, historians, like others, should probably employ traditional forms of textualization, because a radical form of the medium tends to distract the audience from the intended message."[23] Which is presumably why Berkhofer's own book, while calling for genre experiments and criticizing mainstream history for its spurious claims to objectivity, is itself neither "dialogic" nor "polyphonic", but a fairly straightforward and authoritative (if not authoritarian) account.

One field where the interests of (some) historians seem to coincide with those of novelists is "alternate history" (or "allohistory" or "uchronian history"), i.e. accounts, mostly but not exclusively novels, where some historical events are supposed to have happened differently or not at all.[24] Examples are: England bypasses the reformation and remains Catholic; the Confederacy wins the American Civil War; Axis powers are victorious in WW II. (Such "counterfactuals" have actually been used by deadly serious historians as well – e.g. to calculate what difference it would have done to American industrialization if the railway had never been invented and canals had gone on being used. The answer is: surprisingly little.)[25]

These were a few examples of historians relaxing from the supposedly strict rules of the guild. It does not change the fact that historians in general still insist that it is possible to describe and analyze past events and societies, though they are increasingly aware of the necessity to accept that interpretations will vary with the perspective of the historian.

Of late they have even revived something which postmodernists thought had been buried for good – metanarratives. These "Great Stories", which in both their Enlightenment and marxist varieties emphasized human progress towards a sort of utopia, have been much maligned by postmodernists, and for half a century – from c. 1920 to c. 1970 – academic historians actually tended to agree with them. The requirements of empirical accuracy and completeness made it impossible to produce macrohistory which conformed to professional standards, so the larger syntheses were left to "amateurs" and "prophets" like Oswald Spengler and Arnold Toynbee. Marxism on the other hand, while accepting macrohistory as both possible and necessary, in practice was so bound by prevailing orthodoxies that they too failed to produce anything worthwhile. But from c. 1970 there has been a spectacular boom in the writing of macrohistorical syntheses, initiated by but now by no means confined to (non-orthodox) marxists.[26]

Predictably the postmodernist reaction has been one of incredulity that so much historical sociology still dealt with traditional topics like "state-making, the rise of capitalism, comparative political development, revolutions and so on", and that new world histories were published

> by leading British sociologists, seeking presumably to recapture the memories of their grammar school (or perhaps public school) history syllabus… This creates an interesting juxtaposition. On the one hand, the radical diagnoses of the "postmodern condition" are proclaiming the demise of all master narratives; on the other hand, the most ambiguous historical sociologists are defining their project by producing… a new range of grand narratives.[27]

But it is important to stress that it is precisely not a new master narrative, but a range of interpretations that are now being offered. Indeterminacy has crept in even here:

> Everyone understands that these questions [why some nations are rich and some poor] can never be answered in a definitive way, comparable to proving Fermat's Last Theorem. The distribution of prosperity is hopelessly "overdetermined". There are far too many answers that all seem to be right. Culture, geography, institutions, war, religion, and even historical accidents all seem to have played a role. But *what* role, and which factors are most important, remain matters of controversy.[28]

So, in conclusion, historians will probably continue to write their "narratives of remembrance" – seeing it as their task to ensure the existence of a human memory bank, and to offer tentative stories about how humanity evolved from hunting and gathering societies to the global industrial and information society of today.[29] And they will continue to see themselves as different from narrators of fiction. Writing history certainly requires imagination and use of narrative conventions, but a historical work is not only, and not even primarily, a work of literature. As one of the greatest historians (and greatest stylists) realized:

> For the losses of history are indeed irretrievable: when the productions of fancy or science have been swept away, new poets may invent, and new philosophers may reason; but if the one single fact be once obliterated, it can never be restored by the united efforts of Genius and industry.[30]

Notes

1. Joyce Appleby, Lynn Hunt & Margaret Jacob, *Telling the truth about history* (London, 1994), 201-2. – The annotation has been kept to a minimum. The titles mentioned should provide further guidance in the debate. Assuming part of my audience to be Danish, some references will be to books or articles in that language.
2. Richard J. Evans, *In defence of history* (London 1997). More alarmist titles were Keith Windschuttle, *The killing of history: how literary critics and social theorists are murdering our past* (London, 1997; 1st [Australian] ed., 1994); Bryan D. Palmer, *Descent into discourse: the reification of language and the writing of social history* (Philadelphia 1990).
3. Robert F. Berkhofer, Jr., *Beyond the Great Story: history as text and discourse* (Cambridge, Mass., 1995), 1-3.
4. As James Callaghan famously said when the Scottish National Party brought

the Labour government down in 1974, and was close to being annihilated in the following elections. The later trajectory of the SNP might of course give some grounds for hope.
5. Hans Hauge, "Historiens vendinger – sproglige, litterære, pragmatiske", *Den jyske historiker*, no. 50 (1990), 9-27.
6. Geoff Eley, "Is all the world a text? From social history to the history of society two decades later", in: Terrence J. McDonald, ed., *The historic turn in the human sciences* (Ann Arbor, 1996), 214.
7. Terry Eagleton, *The illusions of postmodernism* (1996); Frederic Jameson, *Postmodernism, or the cultural logic of late capitalism* (Durham, N.C. 1991).
8. All quotes from Berkhofer, *Beyond the Great Story*, 234-35.
9. Jonathan Culler, *Literary theory: a very short introduction* (1997), ch. 1; Barbara Epstein, "Postmodernism and the left", *New Politics* 6:2 = no. 22 (1997).
10. Windschuttle, *Killing of history*, 5-6.
11. John Ellis, *Against deconstruction* (London, 1989); C. McCullagh, *The truth of history* (London, 1998); Finn Collin, *Social construction* (London, 1998); Hilary Putnam, *Renewing philosophy* (London, 1992).
12. See most recently Terence Cave, "The strangely neglected ground in the middle", *Times Literary Supplement* (January 15, 1999), 27, a review of Antoine Compagnon, *Le démon de la théorie: littérature et sens commun* (Paris, 1998).
13. This debate is easily accessible on the Internet via Alan Sokal's homepage. It is worthwhile comparing Sokal's hoax with the texts produced randomly by the *Postmodernism generator*, also available on the net. (*http://www.cs.monash.edu.au/links/postmodern.html*)
14. Eley, "Is all the world a text", 215.
15. Keith Thomas, *History and literature* (Swansea, 1988), is an excellent brief discussion (but difficult to obtain). Two Danish articles are strongly recommended: Helge Paludan, "Cairos røde rose: noget om historikernes kildebegreb", *Den jyske historiker*, no. 50 (1990), 29-39, and Steen Busck, "Historie og sandhed", *ibid.*, 41-53.
16. Hayden White, *Metahistory: the historical imagination in nineteenth century Europe* (Baltimore, 1973). It is discussed by Hans Hauge, "Historiens vendinger", and (with more insight) by Jan Pedersen, "Metahistorie", *Historisk tidsskrift* 91 (1991), 526-34.
17. Keith Thomas, *loc.cit.*, 24. Hayden White looked at "pre-modern" historians like Burckhardt, Michelet and de Tocqueville, who might of course be considered more "literary" than their twentieth-century heirs; but that it is in fact possible to apply White's analysis to modern historical works, has been demonstrated by Jan Pedersen i "Historiens form: en sammenligning af tre versioner af Danmarks økonomiske og sociale historie ca. 1750-1810", *Fortid og nutid*, 1998, nr. 3, 181-218.
18. Hayden White, "The question of narrative in contemporary historical theory", *The content of the form: narrative discourse and historical representation* (Baltimore, 1987); Lionel Gossman, "The rationality of history", *Between his-*

tory and literature (Cambridge, Mass., 1990), quote on p. 303. Cf. *Information*, 22.2.1999.
19. See Ansgar Nünning, "'Der historische Roman ist erstens Roman und zweitens keine Historie': Abgrenzung narrativ-fiktionaler Geschichtsdarstellung von der Historiographie", *Von historischer Fiktion zu historiographischer Metafiktion*, vol. 1 (Trier, 1995), 129-205.
20. See Keith Thomas, *History and literature*, 25-27, on the description of British army life in David Lodge's *Ginger, you're barmy* and Steen Busck, "Historie og sandhed" (n. 15) on Skjoldborg's evocation of life among the rural underclass in 19th century Denmark. See also the eleven volumes in the series "Humanistisk historieformidling", recently published by Roskilde Universitetsforlag.
21. Simon Schama, *Dead certainties (Unwarranted speculations)* (London, 1991). On the use of literary conventions in historiography, see Allan Megill & Donald McCloskey, "The rhetoric of history", in: Nelson, J. et al. ed., *The rhetoric of the human sciences: language and argument in scholarship and public affairs* (Madison, Wis. 1987), and Philippe Carrard, *Poetics of the New History: French historical discourse from Braudel to Chartier* (Baltimore, 1992).
22. It is interesting that similar experiments by Jonathan Spence in his work on Chinese history, e.g. *Emperor of China: self-portrait of K'ang-hsi* (London, 1974) and *The death of woman Wang* (London, 1978) have failed to get nearly the same attention.
23. Berkhofer, *Beyond the Great Story*, 357, n. 104.
24. *The Usenet Alternate History List* will give an idea of how rich this field has become: http://www.panix.com/~rbs/AH [990115].
25. My favourite is "The Catholic wind" by the English historian (and later Liberal Democrat education spokesman in the House of Lords) Conrad Russell, in the anthology *For want of a horse: choice and chance in history*, ed. John M. Merriman (Lexington, Mass., 1978). Tongue in cheek and totally deadpan, Russell – a leading expert on 17th century British history – not only describes how William of Orange failed to land in England in 1688 (so that the Glorious Revolution never took place and James II re-Catholized England), but also explains why this was the only conceivable outcome, and why serious historians must therefore dismiss as a figment of the imagination all counterfactual speculations about what might have happened if William had succeeded...
26. Among the most important titles are: Perry Anderson, *Lineages of the absolutist state* (London, 1974); Immanuel Wallerstein, *The modern world-system* (London, 1974 ff.); E. L. Jones, *The European miracle* (London, 1981) and *Growth recurring* (London, 1988); Eric Wolf, *Peoples without history* (London, 1982); Michael Mann, *The sources of social power* (London, 1986); Joel Mokyr, *The lever of riches: technological creativity and economic progress* (London, 1990); Jared Diamond, *Guns, germs and steel: the fates of human societies* (1997, sv. udg. 1999); David Landes, *The wealth and poverty of nations* (London, 1998); F. Fernandez-

Armesto, *Millennium* (London, 1995, da. udg. 1997); R. Bin Wong, *China transformed: historical change and the limits of European experience* (London, 1997), W. L. Runciman, *A treatise of social theory* (3 vols., London, 1983-97), Philip Pomper, ed., *World history: ideologies, structures and identities* (London, 1998). Recent additions include Philip Curtis, *The World and the West* (London, 2000) and Kenneth Pomoranz *The Great Divergence* (Princeton UP, 2000).
27. Geoff Eley, "Is all the world a text?", 206-07.
28. Joel Mokyr, "Secrets of success", *Reason magazine*, December 1998. *http://www.reasonmag.com/9812/bk.mokyr/html* [990115]. Cf. J. R. Rasmussen, "Bringing the world (back) in: global history in the United States", in Stein Tønnesson et al., ed., *Between national histories and global history* (Helsinki, 1997), 23-37.
29. I notice that the writing of literary history seems to be back in fashion, cf. the articles by Jonathan Bate, Andrew Sanders and Ronald Carter & John McRae in *The European English Messenger* VII:2 (Autumn 1998), 12-27. Bate is editing the forthcoming *Oxford English literary history*; Sanders and Carter/MacRae have recently written each their one-volume history.
30. Edward Gibbon, "An Address &c" (1793), in: *The English essays of Edward Gibbon*, ed. Patricia B. Craddock (London, 1972), 535.

Capturing the Present that is Flitting away from us

Marianne Børch

> The point of view in which this tale comes under the Romantic definition lies in the attempt to connect a bygone time with the very present that is flitting away from us.
> Nathaniel Hawthorne, Preface to *The House of Seven Gables*; and epigraph to Antonia Byatt's *Possession: A Romance*.

The subject of this essay is remembrance in modern British literature. In response to the American author Nathaniel Hawthorne's enigmatic words – some found in the title – about romances capturing the present through evoking the past, it will first inquire into the possibility of writing romance today. But there are, of course, other literary modes than romance that seek to capture the elusive moment. In the second part, after a brief, and it is to be hoped not irrelevant, excursion into old literature's constructions of the past, the essay will turn to a writer representative of many who seek to preserve diversified records of events, past and present, write or rewrite memories suppressed or tragically forgotten, and warn against the dangers inherent in such suppression or forgetfulness. The reception of particular historical events lies outside the scope of this essay, which concentrates rather upon the phenomenon of remembrance itself, upon ways of thinking about what memory, and specifically literary memory, is, and what kinds of formal treatment memory invites. Narratives of remembrance, then, are the subject of this essay, but in considering the nature and forms of such narratives, the present writer will of course be offering *her* narrative of recent British literature on or as remembrance, determined by the fact that her principal field of study is literature written before 1800. That slanted perpective is here embraced rather than abandoned, and for two reasons: first, to suggest that familiarity with old texts may be a good basis for the study of later ones; and secondly, in acknowledgement of the fact that any perspective has its limitations, to advertise the particular bias of the present text.

Individuals create identities by narrating their past; you know who you are if you know who you were: Both the fact and some of its implications are evoked by Scots Alasdair Gray in his novel *A History Maker*: We are in a future world (ab. year 2200) where, under the glare of the public eye, Scots tribes conduct constant battles, and where survivors are recovered and mended, as the protagonist finds:

> "You can mend them?" he asked in a voice shrill with unbelief.
> "Mibby. Perhaps. It will take years but they're just lads."
> "Mirren. Most of Charlie's head is gone."
> "He'll grow a new one if we can restore the heart. The new brain will have his character if not his memories."
> "Our memories *are* our character, Mirren."
> "Then the mothers and sisters who love him will restore his memories, Wat Dryhope. We'll give him back all the good things the war sliced away, but *you* won't be one of them, Wattie! When he starts thinking again we'll only remind him of what's harmless!"[1]

So, identity is memory. But as Gray makes clear in this conversation, remembrances can be manipulated. That the memory is a manipulative faculty even without a Mirren's deliberate editing is well suggested by the poet William Stafford:

> So, the world happens twice –
> once we see it as it is;
> second, it legends itself deep,
> the way it is.[2]

– where "legends" suggests both the narrative and mythologizing functions of memory.

Also national identities are "legended," i.e. mythologized. The albatros of historical objectivity having been shot down by Hayden White, words like "memory" and "remembrance" have increasingly appeared in the academic forum in acknowledgement of the "interested" quality of historical explanations, of the way history starts in the now, is dictated by the now's interests, and will be narrated through rhetorical tropes that reflect such interests.[3]

Where history never quite abandons pretensions to objectivity (there are all those unwieldy facts), objectivity has never been the particular forte of literary history. Even so, the discipline seems to be undergoing a transformation rather similar to that of history. *Is Literary History Possible?* asks one theorist, David Perkins, and showing how rigged and manipulated any such history *has* to be, he answers No![4] His position is indirectly affirmed by Patricia Waugh in her literary history of the last 3o to 35 years, *Harvest of the Sixties*: Not only does she rule out "any deistic perspective upon events",[5] Waugh even makes the whole story contingent upon herself:

> To write an account of a historical period through which one has lived is in some sense to write an autobiography where the past and future are necessarily and often mysteriously shaped by the writer's present situation...[6]

Waugh writes literary history as autobiography and views literature as imaginative history. Categories collapse, literature, after a manner, being swallowed up in victory – its own, as it happens. Indeed, Waugh suggests that if history is a narrative project anyway, why not go further and view a period's fiction as its most valid historical record?

> Perhaps contemporary histories can only ever and at best be fragmented autobiographies. If so, then there is a curious logic in reading the age through its imaginative literature.[7]

It is thought-provoking that only "good faith" separates Waugh's position from that of Mr Sludge, the Medium, a character in one of Robert Browning's dramatic monologues. In a passage which Antonia Byatt adopts as one of her epigraphs for her novel *Possession* – the other is Hawthorne's definition of romance cited above – Mr Sludge equates his spiritualist deceptions with those of poet and historian:

> What makes his case out, quite ignores the rest.
> It's a History of the World, the Lizard Age,
> The Early Indians, the Old Country War,

> Jerome Napoleon, whatsoever you please.
> All as the author wants it. Such a scribe
> You pay and praise for putting life in stones.

We should ask such historians, says Sludge,

> 'How many lies did it require to make
> The portly truth you here present us with?'[8]

Waugh never pretends that history will be able to escape its "textuality," but in fact takes a favourable view of Mr. Sludge's literary-historical creativity:

> Perhaps the greatest virtue in approaching a period through its literature is that literary texts have always indirectly connected and confronted paradigmatic contradictions, fraying the trimmed and well-groomed positivistic account of history as a series of formulated periods or a unilinear chain of moments of crisis.[9]

Thus Waugh's tribute to writers for their critique of official narratives – for instance, of a scientific, objectivist historical reliance upon causality and probability. Of course, the present-day loss of confidence in objectivity is accompanied by a loss of faith in straight-line causal explanations, usually inseparable from progressivism. Such progressivism has always, rather paradoxically, gone along with a postulated glorious originating moment, so that, in between miraculous beginning and the destiny embryonically contained in it, we may construct a most satisfying continuous narrative. At present, however, instead of cause and effect and smooth progression, explanatory models offer up chance, catastrophe, leaps, disruptions, overlappings, simultaneity; and the idea of establishing a unified perspective or coherent narrative, diachronic or synchronic, appears quixotic.

But at least we can trust the subject! Or can we? Or may we even? History has been rendered contingent upon the collective or individual rememberer – including the nation-maker and the close observer of historical developments. As regards national identity, traditional narratives of a shared past have been increasingly undermined; not only has the desire-born literariness of all myths of origin been acknowledged; but an influx of increasingly articulate "ethnic" British citizens after the dissolution of the Empire, and loudmouthed protest from various "fringes", have exposed the national narrative of the British as too exclusive. At the personal, epistemological level, the unity of the perceiving individual has of course been questioned: Foucault has famously declared the conceptual pair of "man" and "history" an obsolete construct, and even less radical thinkers find Descartes's *cogitation* less self-evidently valid with every passing day. Cognition and consciousness cannot be held within logical, coherent narratives: significant personal break-throughs, for instance, will be unpredictable, not gradual or the result of systematic discovery. "One's intelligence may march about and about a problem but the solution does not come gradually into view. One moment it is not. The next it is there," as a character says in Golding's *Rites of Passage*.[10] Self-perceptions, moreover, do not gather into a unified self, and Antonia Byatt represents many British writers' concern with the constructedness of personal identity, the apparent fact that it is something you make, not something you have. Her modern heroine Maud ruefully asks: "who am I? A matrix for susurration of texts and codes?",[11] while the narrator observes that

> it may seem odd to begin a description of Roland Michell with an excursus into the complicated relations between Blackadder, Cropper and Ash, but it was in these terms Roland most frequently thought of himself. When he did not think in terms of Val.[12]

Byatt's character Ellen, the frigid wife of the nineteenth-century poet Ash, dramatises the author's awareness that the task of constructing a personality involves exclusion, and often exclusion of perceptions, or images, that can be remembered, but never verbalized, and so leave behind only absences and texts edited by silence.

The optimistic potential of the perhaps rather depressing idea of personality as a bric-a-brac do-it-yourself construct is tirelessly explored by another contemporary novelist, Jeanette Winterson, who glories in the mercurial self, exploring the roads not taken as well as those that may be taken at the concrete level of one particular life. Thus, in *Oranges are not the only Fruit*,[13] the budding self of Jeanette *is*, in a sense, the sensitive and searching Sir Percival as well as the princess of fairy tales. The versatile manifestations of Winterson's characters are made possible by a narrative universe that obeys the latest theories of time and space: In a list of seven lies in *Sexing the Cherry*, we find "Time is a straight line;" "The difference between the past and the future is that one happened while the other has not;" and "We can only be in one place at a time."[14] Winterson's paradigmatic *space* is Venice, where

> Although wherever you are going is always in front of you, there is no such thing as straight ahead. No as the crow flies short cut will help you reach the café just over the water.[15]

But Winterson's many identities are created not only in different persons across history and space, but also consecutively in one individual, where revolutionary breaks interrupt oppressive continuity. In *Oranges*, the author invents her protagonist's origin three times over (even apart from her fairy tale analogues): from her birth through her foster moster's adoption to her true birth on the discovery of her sexual identity; moreover, she invents for each stage its particular mythology of origin – there is birth through sexual union, birth through immaculate conception, and finally self- or interactive birth through erotic awakening. Here we have a writer who graphically confirms Waugh's claim that the ego has become "a narrative project".[16]

But there is still the body. Maud's speculations about the self in *Possession* – already cited – continue:

> There was the question of the awkward body. The skin, the breath, the eyes, the hair, *their history, which did seem to exist*.[17]

Winterson's novel *Written on the Body*,[18] suggestively titled, documents the body as a remembering entity, an archaeological site full of traces of the past. The intense concern among contemporary writers and critics with the body obviously responds not only to questions of gender, but to an epistemological question as urgent as it is comical, namely how to get rid of the notion of the individual with the body so obstinately, and unacademically, refusing to dissolve even under the corrosive breath of French philosophers.

So, perhaps we are allowed to keep the body. Still, with the disruption of the Newtonian universe, with connections and cognition a matter of leaps and bounds rather than of continuity and logic, the very possibility of narrative, dependent upon some consistency of viewpoint, some meaningful notion of character, and some temporal continuity, seems threatened.

But narrative and narrators are not easily defeated. The romances of Byatt and Winterson, for instance, assert that a personality can be created, *and* created in a dialogue with the past that, although stone-dead, can live precisely in the very flitting present that is itself unavailable for scrutiny.

Possession presents a narrative pattern commonly found in contemporary works. Two plots: one past, one contemporary; they are connected, but not by simple causality; discovery of a family bond between past and present is barely relevant given its context of much more mysterious affinities.

Nor is there any simple connection between the book's two male protagonists a century apart. Both Ash and Roland are in quest of an identity, and in both cases an identity is achieved partly through the love affair so central to romance, partly through an intimate, romantic engagement with the past, or more precisely, past texts. What disrupts the stale lives of poet and poet-to-be, then, are strange women and strange old poems and tales. Such strangeness initiates quests that create the questers. From the outset, Byatt dramatises the way past awakens present even as present discovers past. Newly found, Ash's old letters, "tied about and about, like a mummy" stir into life, producing a "kind of rustling and shifting, enlivened by their release";[19] and the moment is so exciting for Roland that it effects a stirring in his dead emotions and, indeed, in his body, so that he is able to go through with sexual intercourse he has looked forward to with dismay.

This scene, showing how past pricks up present, strikes the keynote for the rest. Uncovering – or almost uncovering – the mystery of Ash's life – a life that at the outset seemed over-documented – Roland finds that his own character has been rigidly constructed around a delusion and is free to create himself. At the end, finally new-born as himself, a poet, he enters the world of death and the process that is history.

The distinction between process and stasis is crucial also for Jeanette Winterson, whose views of the relation between history and story are inseparable from her conception of character.

> We make [stories] what we will. It's a way of explaining the universe while leaving the universe unexplained, it's a way of keeping it alive, not boxing it into shape. Everyone who tells a story tells it differently, just to remind us that everybody sees it differently.[20]

History, in contrast, is the English myth of St. George; history is Jeanette's ever-certain mother, who can accommodate anything within her evangelical vision; the best historian of all is Pol Pot, who destroyed all records that might problematize his/story. History is always a legitimising and unifying myth, exemplary and grand, full of national heroes and abstractions; whereas the notion of story (the locus for individual expression) is conveyed in an almost bathetically "low" metaphor: story is that most common of British foods, a sandwich, something to pass through the digestive system, something that builds the person, something everybody eats but will be compiled according to individual taste, laced with mustard of one's own.[21]

Jeanette's mustard is sharp and her digestion strong. She creates herself and her story out of history in so radical a manner that her world – her historical context – must call her rebirth demonic. Byatt's account of Roland's "birth" in *Possession*, as he enters in a garden of Eden on the first day of the world, suggests transformation rather than revolution. Byatt optimistically envisions poetic awakening as a liberation from past tropes and myths of origin that in fact recreates and so perpetuates them.[22]

Still, *Possession* has constantly *problematized* myths of origin as well as the concept of historical truth. The characters' search for *the* truth about Ash is related to their desire for an ordered, single meaningful narrative, and when they find such a narrative, it is satisfying, but defective. Not even new discoveries can ever complete the edited journal of Ash's wife or bring Blanche Glover's marginalised existence to the centre. Moreover, the reader is allowed access to historical information withheld from the protagonists, who thus construct their satisfying connection with the past upon a foundation of some truths, some fabrications, and some exclusions. Where Winterson uninhibitedly celebrates the artful reconstruction of past identities, Byatt, also intent upon celebrating the miraculous contact between past and present, inscribes the – predominantly epistemological, but also social – problems of establishing such a link.

By making sleazy Mr Sludge the true tutelary spirit of the romance in which she captures present through narrating past, Byatt acknowledges the relevance of objections to the genre raised or implied by other writers. One such writer would be John Fowles, who makes it his business to deny his readers the pleasure of mirroring themselves in the past. In *A Maggot*,[23] we again find a double plot and an undefined relation with the past, but mirror effects or causal explanations are precluded as a story attempts to reach us from an alien past, but cannot quite surface at the level of modern narration. An intrusive narrator keeps explaining in modern vocabulary the customs and objects and old words of the narrative, the semantic difference between words shared; imagery is outrageously anachronistic; long present-tense sequences detail past action that refuses to structure itself for a modern audience – we see, but do not understand; cuttings from eighteenth-century periodicals speak of a barbarous age we would not want to make our mirror, thus challenging a reader either to revise his favourable self-image and acknowledge that remembering the past offers untenable temptations of beautifying the present; or to deny that ideas of historical continuity as well as the concept of a "mankind" are really meaningful constructs.[24]

Formally, Fowles indicates the inability of past and present to mirror, evoke, or "create" each other by abrupt stylistic and structural leaps. Byatt and Winterson, who argue that past and present *can* touch, both commit themselves to formal features of romance. Here, Byatt is quite traditional, using a classical "interlace" pattern to puppetteer a vast and motley crowd of characters along their progress; whereas Winterson develops her interlace pattern by making the individual strands of plot so many different enactments of the possible identities and choices of her central protagonist: With her triple or spiral patterns, parallels between present and past, and even moments when past and present intersect, Winterson seems almost to be moving towards an apocalyptic abandonment of a historical perspective. Crudely, one might say that Fowles is resolutely historicist; Byatt depicts history transcended, but subverts transcendence by a number of narrative and generically signalled reservations; Winterson breaks the historical framework completely.

The three authors' different choices with respect to language support such a distinction: Fowles creates two languages so incompatible that he has to keep translating one into the other. Byatt is a masterly re-creator of a nineteenth-century conceptual and idiomatic world as different, yet insists that investigating its meaning, moderns come to understand both it and themselves: past *may* meet present. Winterson's apocalytic vision demands a modern language, the old made new, and, after her (alter ego's) explosive eruption into a self, confidently reassembles the scattered debris of a meticulously researched tradition entirely as it suits her.

Where some writers cast a critical eye upon romancing narratives of remembrance, many have actively shunned romance to turn their gaze upon the real world. This is especially true of authors interested less in the individual than in the social self, in groups and nations, in questions of gender and race.

Conventional wisdom of literary history has long depicted the author's progress from the heart of society – as society's memory, historian, poet, and mythologizer, alike – towards the margins, and finally outside of relevance altogether. Today, the tide might have turned. When authors are looking into the world, there are eyes looking back. There are authors who display a strong commitment to a public role, not as ideologues in a narrow sense, but in showing a concern with questions of knowledge and social realities that meet with understanding and sympathy in a community where the explosion of technological media, for one thing, has made questions of cognition, for instance the understanding of time and space, everyone's constant preoccupation. Perhaps there is among the reading public a common dissatisfaction with the very ideas that over several hundred years have increasingly marginalized authors for their critique of official truths, a critique that Patricia Waugh views as the defining quality of the writer's art. I should like to repeat her point, since it is the one universalist myth that is allowed to remain in her critical universe:

> *Writers have always* confronted paradigmatic contradictions ...

Looking back through centuries when today's expiring Enlightenment culture was shaped, writers have, indeed, connected and confronted paradigmatic contradictions, and if not fraying, then at least tearing at, trimmed and well-fitted accounts of history.

Beginning with the conception of character as continuous memory starting from a moment of origin, a writer like Lawrence Sterne questions the notion of a coherent personality as well as the assumption of an original moment as source and explanation, as the heaping up of all-significant causes of Tristram Shandy's disorganized memory destroys the significance of any one cause. Sterne demolishes John Locke's explanations from inside by this reductio ad absurdum-technique and implicitly demands broader explanations, in fact looking back to times that had room for catastrophe, miracle, whim, and God. Sterne and his ilk – he wasn't alone – are admittedly flighty-minded gentlemen; but a seeming contrast like matter-of-fact Daniel Defoe, equally, from his politico-social perspective, questions myths of unified and continuous origin. In a *True-Born Englishman* (1701), Defoe demonstrates how a group's self-understanding and power in the present are upheld by the myths of its collective memory, and spitefully demolishes the myth of a unified, racially pure origin for the English. After 428 angry lines, he concludes that "A Turkish Horse can show more History,/ To prove his well-descended family" than can an Englishman.[25] Here Defoe does to national identity what Sterne is to do to the individual consciousness.

But then again, are these two writers representative in their historical paradigm-fraying activities? Sterne was highly idiosyncratic, Defoe a subversive upstart. But they *are* representative! If one looks at national identity, Defoe differs from celebrators of national myths in his eagerness to explode them rather than in regarding as false what they hold true. In fact, even pre-Enlightenment historians are much less naïvely accepting of English myths of origin than often assumed. In 1485, the first English printer, William Caxton, publishes Malory's Arthurian matter, the *Morte D'Arthur*, expressly to boost the unity of a war-torn English nation. Caxton admits that quite possibly Arthur never existed; he cites various "evidences" that he might have done – evidence none too impressive, however, and Caxton in fact ends by making it clear that he does not finally *care* about the verifiable truth of his history: "to give faith and believe all is true that is contained herein, ye be at your liberty".[26] He clearly accepts his material as historically true for pragmatic reasons: His myth is history because histories are narratives of necessary remembrance for a nation, and this is the collective memory England needs to have.

I end this brief historical review with my personal favourite Geoffrey Chaucer not to pile up instances of past writers' self-consciously pragmatic views of history, but because Chaucer makes a point about history as remembrance that is tied to *his* historical moment, but has acquired new relevance today. It has to do with the way modes of transmission impinge upon remembrance.

His most famous work, *the Canterbury Tales*, was written when England was passing from an oral to a literate culture, and presents itself as a series of tales told, remembered, and written down, a narrative strategy rich in implications for our subject.[27] One character, the Wife of Bath, is famous for her subversive opinions about sex and the nature of power, but her treatment of history is no less subversive. Her tale is the only Chaucerian text that takes up England's great Arthurian myth: The first lines place us back in that golden age, which turns out to have been a dangerous time, when elves and other incubi lay ambushed, ready to jump upon maidens and implant their demonic seed in them. Thank God, rejoices the Wife, today we have no such fairies, for they have been exorcised and then replaced by all those nice monks, whose bastard brood will surely be a blessing! A pseudo-enlightened present is thus at once set against a benighted past. The tale that follows depicts an Arthurian knight who starts by committing rape, who continues to behave abominably throughout, and still is allowed to live happily ever after. Again, the good old days are exposed as a hollow myth, and the mirror set up between past and present produces not Snow-White's congratulatory self-image, but mutual exposure.

Chaucer's fiction is interesting in my context not just for the Wife of Bath's deflationary historicism, but especially for the fact *that we can read it*. The text, occupying a gap between spoken and written, in fact sets down an iconoclastic viewpoint that an oral culture would necessary "forget," i.e. elide. As Chaucer takes over the oral poet's function of remembering and possessing tradition, he frequently reflects upon the problems of a coalescence between individual memory and a community's history: sole carrier of tradition, the bard's version is *the* version, and each new version destroys the former to produce an ever-changing, yet always single and uncontestable story, which will always be that of the dominant group. An oral society elides diversity, where writing allows for multiple representations, multiple memories.

This is a point worth repeating today. I have looked back in history to substantiate Waugh's "writers have always" (with stress on *always*), but also in order to argue for special emphasis upon the word *writers* as against oral narratives, which do *not* problematize official paradigms of truth in a historically significant manner – by which I mean they can have no impact upon the future.

The danger inherent in the "oral" text is implied by Tony Harrison in his response to the Gulf War, which, as we know, was a highly edited war. In the midst of the clinical cleanliness, *The Observer* printed a picture of a charred Iraqi soldier, a trace someone had forgotten to erase. The author Geoff Dyer finds photographs a crucial factor in remembrance, when voices have been silenced:

> Theodor Adorno said famously that there would be no poetry after Auschwitz. Instead, he failed to add, there would be photography.[28]

It is a good point, but the question is just *how* a picture speaks. The 1996 exhibition of photos taken seconds before the Cambodian persons they remind us of were executed say so little; the shocking thing is how inexpressive they are, and that the strong emotion evoked derives from one's knowledge of context rather than from the pictures. These photos speak, but have no voice; what they do, I think, is indicate a silence; pictures like that of the charred Iraqi soldier may go further and claim a voice, perhaps because context is so graphically inscribed in their still or still(ed) lives. The poet and novelist Helen Dunmore saw the same picture, also needed to speak, and also pondered the way photos speak:

> That killed head straining through the windscreen
> with its frill of bubbles in the eye-sockets
> is not trying to tell you something –
>
> it is telling you something.[29]

Harrison notes the windscreen wiper in the picture, and reading it as a sign of intended communication, a pen lifted, but intercepted before the soldier's legacy was written down, the poet has undertaken to give him his voice back.

But it is no easy task. Much has been done to suppress that voice. Moreover, the silent mask is too horrible for empathy. And finally, even successful empathy introduces a danger – that of a colonizing perspective.[30]

That Harrison rejects condescending empathy is suggested already at the narrative level: The dead soldier's speech is largely an injunction not to mythologize his fate in a way that legitimises the Western attack by rewriting his memories:

> 'Lie and pretend that I excuse
> my bombing by B52s
> …
> Pretend I've got the imagination
> to see the world beyond one nation.'[31]

He knows what poets are – liars. He has not, in fact, picked out the poet to be interpreted, but to have his own words recorded on his tape recorder:

> 'Don't be afraid I've picked on you
> for this exclusive interview.
>
> Isn't it your sort of poet's task
> to find words for this frightening mask?
>
> If that gadget that you've got records
> words from such scorched vocal chords,
>
> press RECORD before some dog
> devours me mid-monologue.'[32]

We laugh rather nervously at the bad taste or at the sarcasm. Self-defensive laughter is, indeed, almost the only way in which Harrison allows the western reader to negotiate his relation with the soldier, whose speech remains hostile and highly mannered – sarcastic, full of very clever jibes and puns and playing upon technical, Greek-derived, tongue-tripping, funny-sounding terms, colloquial one second, mock-formal the next, often awfully, precisely awfully comic – but also comically inadequate to the tragedy which literally *no one* can understand; although Harrison's impersonation does manage radically to dismember the clichés with which horror might be frozen into a comfortingly memorialised form.

Not least effective are the understatements, the polite discourse that will bridge the gap between enemies, between strangers in a linguistic analogue to no-man's-land: Arguing how war breeds war, while single nationalist perspectives obscure the dangers of war, the dead face apologetically curbs his passion, "(excuse a skull's sarcastic manner!)";[33] afraid to lose his audience, he adopts the urbanity of "unfriendly":

> 'Don't look away! I know it's hard
> to keep regarding one so charred,
>
> so disfigured by *unfriendly* fire
> and think it once burned with desire.'[34]

The euphemistic understatement, Harrison's choice to abstain from overly cherché and abstruse difficulty, his choice of narrative and dialogue rather than lyrical meditation, and his alternation between fierce invective and urbanity, make his poem hark back to Augustan, eighteenth-century satirical exhortatory discourse, an association the poet appears to encourage with his iambic rhymed couplets reminiscent of the preferred satirical metre of the Augustans (though Harrison employs tetrameter rather than pentameter). This artificial discourse, that of a truce for negotiating hostile relations, avoids the colonisation mentioned above: enemies remain enemies: Iraqi soldier hates Englishman, the Englishman does not sentimentalise his Iraqi enemy. Meanwhile, there is a clear attack on the practice of silencing one narrative so as to elevate another to *the* truth; insisting upon the alienness of the man he speaks for, Harrison also insists upon the right of that alien perspective to be articulated, even in making it clear that his record of the recording is terribly inadequate. But contact of a kind there is. The fabricated memory opens the imagination to the unassimilably alien; an opening which opens for the poet's understanding of another alien world, namely his own past. In the other Gulf War poem, "Initial Illuminations," relics of the past central to British pride and national identity – such as Anglo-Saxon

Eadfrith's illuminations – cease to be understood as mere aesthetic objects, and are re-membered (the inevitable pun!) as a complex record of beauty and violence. Harrison's temporarily adopted pose that the art of i'nitial il,lumi,nations is beautiful, ideology-less, disinterested, is rendered suspect and naïve by the i'nitial il,lumi'nation of the fires lighted over Baghdad.[35] Present here interprets the past, salvages it from dehistoricised irrelevance, and, in sum, reinstates it as memory rather than relic. In the end, the meeting with aliens across time and cultural traditions makes it convincing for Harrison to evoke the highly unfashionable concept of "mankind," with his elegiac note tinged by a highly unfashionable moralism:

> let them remember, all those who celebrate,
> that their good news is someone else's bad
> or the light will never dawn on poor mankind.[36]

Harrison's poeticised encounter with the silenced soldier would seem to illustrate many trends in the way modern writing remembers the past:

First, I have suggested how Harrison writes almost like an Augustan, developing an *urbanity* that enables contact across cultural gaps; in this connection it is interesting to find critic Steven Connor discussing features in modern writings that might reflect *problems of "addressivity"* common to eighteenth-century and twentieth-century writers, who both have to negotiate relations with an unknown and highly diverse readership.[37]

Second, the modern Augustan has a sense of public responsibility. In some writers, this sense mounts from Harrison's wishful imperative – "let those" – to what Steven Connor calls "Dickensian denunciation"[38] or even a "vatic" note, which I find characteristic not only of Margaret Drabble, Connor's occasion for bringing this up, but certainly also of Jeanette Winterson, a modern, self-professed prophet!

Harrison, thirdly, develops a *mannered, mixed style* that naturally avails itself of today's multicultural repertoire, but may also be understood as a defense against discourse types that would capture and domesticate alien voices.

Finally, Harrison *warns against the single perspective*: several narratives are better than one, and *writing* is the preserve of multiple voices, capturing presents otherwise allowed to flit by unremembered.

Harrison's need to restore one voice to the diminished chorus of remembrances of the Gulf War points to the continued relevance of a work that warns against a single-truth, single-memory society, namely George Orwell's *1984*. There, controlled media reproduce an oral stage of society, where "thought-crimes" "include the possession of memory, the desire for records and the creation of connections between past and present;"[39] where the past is changed by the present in a process that, for all the feverish reinvention of history that it involves, actually disguises and denies the fact of change.[40] In *A History-Maker* – quoted at the beginning – Alasdair Gray echoes Orwell's concern as he imagines a future society after the "historical era," where memories may be manipulated and where troublemakers are those who have memories and want to know history.[41]

Suspicion of the single, deistic perspective (whether founded in ideological fiat or epistemological assumption) and of past myths that cultivated such a perspective has led not only to nightmare visions, but also to a proliferation of writings and re-writings that seek to make up for past ages' defective and selective memories. History is rewritten and reimagined, an endeavour which naturally takes up for review the concept of national identity, of "Englishness." Here, one finds alongside a writer like Angus Wilson,[42] immigrant background or mixed-origin writers assisting in the critique and perspectivisation of "Englishness," as in *The Remains of the Day*, where Kazuo Ishiguro almost appears to be doing for a dying conception of Englishness what Harrison has done for the dead Iraqi soldier.[43] Honorary mention is due at this point also to Monty Python and others, who have meekly taken up the new white, and predominantly male, burden of rewriting the old myths and *histories*, dismantling and, indeed, historicising them, tying them to places and times.[44]

In the field of literature, casting off a dead-weight past also means revising the canon – or at least keeping old books on a new critical basis whilst adding texts "forgotten" under old criteria. It also means "devolving" literature, so that London is no longer the understood centre around which all writing in English revolves; finally, it means the creation of texts that make space, as it were, for voices and perspectives counted out under old ideologies – producing memories worth having.[45]

"Worth having" sounds pragmatic and demagogic, of course, but to cite Germaine Greer's opinion, which chimes in perfectly with Caxton's and Defoe's, "[s]imply to *have* a past provides an historicist resource for changing the present."[46] So silenced or ventriloquised groups (women, racially oppressed, colonially marginalized) are now busy *recollecting* their past – in both senses of assembling material and reorganizing it into useful memories – extending the repertoire of origin myths or explanatory models already available. Here discourse problems are often a prominent concern; available languages are felt to carry so many remnants of a colonized and colonizing past, and to lack so many words and necessary idioms, that the struggle for a newly remembered identity involves a decentering and problematization of dominant discourse types, a broadening and stopping of gaps in the language. I shall avoid voluble name-dropping and just mention one work, although it seems unfair that the most representative specimen I can think of is written by a white male – and non-British to boot; but he writes in English, and he rewrites a famous canonical English work. J.M. Coetzee's *Foe* illustrates the fact and nature of the concern with extending the cultural and cognitive ambience – or memory – of the English language that is shared across marginalised groups, as, in imagining the creation of Defoe's *Robinson Crusoe*, he gives voice to a woman who is herself eager to articulate the experience of Man Friday, who in this version is tongueless, speechless, recordless, and so history-less.[47]

I have proceeded throughout as if memory itself did not need definition, although I have problematised both remembrances and remembrancers. In rounding up, I shall briefly refer to a change that may be occurring in the memory function itself under pressure of modern life's multiple simultaneous claims upon the individual's attention; this pressure is felt to bring about what Steven Connor calls "the accelerating amnesia of electronic culture,"[48] a culture where the personality is created in a constant negotiation with contemporary impulses rather than in a continuous relation with one's own, socially constructed past. The reader who wants a hilarious impression of what it is to live with, or in, a mind invaded by the totality of simultaneously available cultural impulses, a mind where memory and history coalesce completely, should read Salman Rushdie's *Midnight's Children*.[49]

The above, in looking for coherence, formal resemblances, and shared authorial impulses has sought to construct a narrative of the many ways in which present-day British writers remember the past and deal with the phenomenon of remembrance.[50] No narrative is without a moral, however, and mine comes in the form of a tribute to books, because they are always new, but also, not least important, because they are always old.

We appear at present to be approaching a quasi-oral stage of society; an increasing amount of attention is given to the spoken word in connection with visual images; simultaneously, computer technology can change texts indefinitely, producing the evolving text in a process which elides the old. This reminds one of that "oral society" which in a global context might introduce the world of *1984*; or, as in Alasdair Gray's comical, weird, and very shrewd vision of the future, produce a new two-nations division, where a tribal quasi-oral culture can be incorporated within a highly organized, global media-controlled world because both kinds of society are history-ridden, yet rest upon a-historical assumptions.[51] One might say that Gray and Orwell evoke worlds that show how awful it would be to live in the present. So, let that flitting moment pass, for heaven's sake, and let us capture it only in con-text, con-texts made up largely of written texts.

Writing (caught in print or manuscript) is self-historicising, subjectivising, inscribed with its own obsolescence; as you write, you consign your word to the past. This obsolescence is one of the true miracles of writing. One impressive feature of Geoffrey Chaucer's writing is his understanding of the cultural changes that create him: he knows that when texts are written down, they will reach a large, and uncontrollably complex audience, where what he calls "auctoritee" – the "authoritive text" or official truth – may acquire dangerous functions. Books, says Chaucer, are indeed the key of remembrance, but not all carry the same authority, and texts should indicate this fact. Recording a significant memory, a dream that he had, Chaucer hands it down to posterity "as *I kan now remembre*".[52] Here every word – I, can, now, remember – undercuts textual authority, or rather ties it securely to an individual. This ploy historicises the text as against the self-updating dynamism of the oral text. It limits the potential for abuse by the writer, who might as well have written *as I will now remembre*. It also makes space for new texts and new subjectivities, and enables new presents to define themselves in a constant process of negotiating their relation with the past whose *difference* is fixed in writing.[53] In other words, the living word lives by being allowed to be dead. Only a dead letter can give live modern readers the relay-point that allows them to understand their present – without getting trapped in it!

Notes

1. Harms: Penguin, 1994, p. 38.
2. Cited by Joyce Carol Oates in "First Principles and 'Transformations of Play'" from *The Life of the Writer and the Life of the Career, New Literary History*, 27, 1996, p. 252.
3. There are those historicists who believe that texts and truths can and should be freed from the stranglehold of the present and seek to place the past back where it came from, in the (different) past. Historicising ventures can, to some extent, appear Quixotic, for although their placing the past securely in the past might demythologise it, this only happens at the price of the relevance without which the past becomes worthless – its truth standing in direct relation to its incomprehensibility. Moreover, in their readiness to forego relevance, historicists must inevitably confront the knowledge that a hermeneutic circle renders the historicised past no less a product of the present than more frankly acknowledged fabrications.
4. Baltimore & London, John Hopkins University Press, 1992.
5. Waugh (Oxford: Oxford UP, 1995), p. 11.
6. Waugh, p. 1.
7. Waugh, p. 2. Linda Hutcheon similarly detects in many recent novels a new attitude towards history that makes it "historiographic metafiction" which combines an undercutting scepticism about the possibility of representing history with a continuing commitment to the attempt itself. *A Poetics of Postmodernism* (London: Routledge, 1988).
8. Hawthorne in the epigraph to this article, and Browning cited from Antonia Byatt, *Possession* (London: Vintage, 1990).
9. Waugh, p. 12. Waugh's approach returns the literary text to a relationship with an historical real that has in the meantime been refashioned in its image; cf. Steven Connor, *The English Novel in History, 1950-1995* (London: Routledge, 1996), p. 131.

10. London, Faber & Faber, 1980, p. 85.
11. *Possession*, p. 251.
12. *Possession*, p. 10.
13. London, Vintage, 1985.
14. London, Vintage, 1989, p. 89.
15. *The Passion* (Harms.: Penguin, 1987), p. 49.
16. Waugh, p. 37.
17. *Possession*, p. 251.
18. London, Jonathan Cape, 1992.
19. *Possession*, pp. 84 and 3 (cf. p. 105).
20. *Oranges are not the only Fruit*, p. 91.
21. *Oranges are not the only Fruit*, p. 93. See also Steven Connor's analysis of digestion as a recurrent metaphor for adaptation without loss of continuity in Timothy Mo's *Sour Sweet* (1982), *The English Novel in History*, p. 100.
22. Byatt's description of Roland's discovery of his poetic voice after a deep sense of belatedness is clearly influenced by Harold Bloom's "anxiety of influence" theory (1973).
23. London, Picador, 1991 (first publ. 1985).
24. One smells the blood of a Frenchman here, Foucault with his *Discipline and Punish*, where history ultimately functions as a countermemory that does lead to modern reflection; and nowhere is the inability to distance the past clearer than in Fowles's own obtrusive design upon the reader, the way *he* imposes *his* vision of the past upon us, *his* construction.
25. *Poems on Affairs of State: Augustan Satirical Verse, 1660-1714*, vol. 6: 1797-1704, ed. Frank Ellis (New Haven: Yale University Press, 1970), pp. 259-309, ll. 227-8.
26. Thomas Malory, *Morte Darthur*, New Oxford Classics, ed. Helen Cooper (Oxford: Oxford UP, 1998), pp. 528-30.
27. *The Riverside Chaucer*, ed. Larry Benson (Oxford: Oxford UP, 1988).
28. *Missing of the Somme* (Harms.: Penguin, 1994), p. 42.
29. "Poem on the Obliteration of 10,000 Iraqi Soldiers," *Recovering a Body* (Newcastle on Tyne: Bloodaxe, 1994), p. 24.
30. A point also made by Helen Dunmore in an "Afterword," where she suggests the danger of seizing "on the sufferings of others in order to express [one's] own sensitivity."
31. Tony Harrison, *A Cold Coming: Gulf War Poems* (Newcastle upon Tyne: Bloodaxe, 1991), "A Cold Coming," ll. 139-40, 151-2.
32. "A Cold Coming," ll. 11-18.
33. "A Cold Coming," l. 130.
34. "A Cold Coming," ll. 97-100.
35. The poem's title is ambiguous, the two meanings of "initial" hinging upon near homonyms distinguished only by different stress patterns. In my text I have suggested the difference between primary (') and secondary (,) strong stress.
36. "Initial Illumination," ll. 25-7.

37. Connor, *The English Novel in History*, p. 164.
38. *The English Novel in History*, p. 61.
39. Connor, *The English Novel in History*, p. 210.
40. Paraphrases Connor, p. 207.
41. *A History-Maker*, p. 108. The Truffaut film *Fahrenheit 451* (1966), based upon Ray Bradbury's novel, depicts an oral culture resolutely hanging on to the written word as a way of maintaining cultural identity under a book-burning tyrannical regime.
42. *Anglo-Saxon Attitudes* (Harms.: Penguin, 1992 [first published 1956]).
43. London, Faber and Faber, 1989.
44. Postwar poets often put on a less hilarious, but still humorously debunking attitude to the remembered past – i.e. that past that their parents talk about, and which gives shape to present policies. Representative are the once-renowned Liverpool Poets, Adrian Henry, "Great War Poems" (see Introduction) and Roger McGough, "Why Patriots are a bit Nuts in the Head" (*The Mersey Sound*, [Harms.: Penguin, 1967], pp. 24 and 73), both of which depict history as bunk in a reality consisting of modest, but available short-term pleasures.
45. On being swallowed by others' history, see Ishmael Reed:
    i am outside of
        history. i wish
        i had some peanuts, it
        looks hungry there in
        its cage.

        i am inside of history. its
        hungrier than i
        thot.
                    'Dualism: in Ralph
                    Ellison's invisible man.'
46. Cited in Paul Hamilton, *Historicism* (London: Routledge, 1996), p. 201.
47. (Harms.: Penguin, 1986). However, Friday has something unavailable to people inhabiting speech, time, and history.
48. *The English Novel in History*, p. 162.
49. London, Picador, 1982.
50. Some commentators feel that the threat of the nuclear big bang that would destroy humanity affects the memory-as-identity construct: How can we backtrack from the unimaginable? Which past can "legend" – i.e. endow with structure and meaning – a present with no future? Novels that have provoked discussion of this issue are, for instance, Maggie Gee's *The Burning Book* (London: Faber and Faber, 1989 [first published 1983]), Anthony Burgess's *The End of the World News* (Harms.: Penguin, 1983); and Russel Hoban's *Riddley Walker* (London: Picador, 1980).
51. In fact, Gray's future world operates with masses of recognisable historical

references, which make the work a virtual Bluff-your-Way-Guide, but all perspectives are foreshortened, fact and fiction mixed, and ideological necessity the central criterion for interpretation.
52. *The House of Fame*, l. 64, cited from *The Riverside Chaucer*.
53. Chaucer's historical awareness makes him not only the almost proverbial "father of English poetry," but in fact father of English literary history. For a discussion which presents and explores this insight, see A.C.Spearing, *Medieval to Renaissance in English Poetry* (Cambridge: Cambridge University, 1985), ch. 2.

The Authors

Helen Dunmore is a poet and novelist. Her books include *Zennor in Darkness* (awarded the McKitterick Prize, 1994), *A Spell of Winter* (which won the Orange Prize for Fiction, 1996), *Your Blue-eyed Boy*, and the poetry collection *The Raw Garden*. Her most recent novel is *Talking to the Dead: A Novel* (1998).

Eve Patten currently lectures in English at Trinity College, Dublin, Ireland. Between 1993 and 1996 she was a lecturer in Irish and British Cultural Studies with the British Council, Bucharest, Romania.

Nils Arne Sørensen is senior lecturer in Modern European History at University of Southern Denmark, Odense. He has published articles and books on British, Danish and Italian history, and is currently doing research on the commemoration of World War I in European border areas.

David McCrone is Professor in Sociology at University of Edinburgh. Among his publications are *Scotland: the Sociology of a Stateless Nation* (1991); *Scotland – the Brand: the Making of Scottish Heritage* (1995) and *Understanding Nationalism: Tomorrow's Ancestors* (1998).

Dr. phil. *Lars Ole Sauerberg* is professor of literature in English at University of Southern Denmark, Odense University. His publications include books and articles on the interface between literature and history. He is is General and English Editor of *Orbis Litterarum*.

Jens Rahbek Rasmussen is senior lecturer in British history and politics, Copenhagen University. Recent publications include *Briterne og Europa* (DUPI, 1997, with Nils Arne Sørensen) and "In defence of society: an historian reflects on British Studies", *Journal for the Study of British Cultures,* 6:1 (1999). Currently working on a study of the image of Britain in Denmark around 1900 and a short history of the British Isles for students of English.

Marianne Børch is associate professor at University of Southern Denmark, Odense, where she teaches and studies, mainly, early literature in English. Her doctoral dissertation (1993) was an attempt to formulate a Chaucerian poetic.